The Dog Who Rescued Me

Jerri Kay Lincoln

Copyright © 2013 Jerri Kay Lincoln

All rights reserved.

Ralston Store Publishing
P.O. Box 1684
Prescott, Arizona 86302

ISBN 978-1-938322-18-1

This book edited by:
Mesa Verde Media Services
www.MesaVerdeMediaServices.com

Printed in the USA.

Out of difficulties, grow miracles.
—Jean de la Breyere

Miracles happen every day. Not just in remote country villages or at holy sites halfway across the globe, but here, in our own lives.
—Deepak Chopra

Sometimes fear is necessary in order for the soul to find its path again.
—Paulo Coelho

I am thankful to all those who said no. It's because of them, I did it myself.
—Albert Einstein

Table of Contents

Prologue	1
Part One: How It All Began	5
Part Two: Happy Tail-Waggin' Times	13
Part Three: Two Lives Lived in Fear	33
Part Four: The End of Life as We Knew It	41
Part Five: Aftermath	45
Part Six: The Healing	55
Epilogue	173
Resources	175

Prologue

This is the story of me and my dog, Moki. The story starts in the middle because you need to know what happened before you know why it happened. You need to know how the miracle came about and how something so horrible turned into something wonderful. What follows is a single life-changing event. The rest of the book tells our story.

On the night it happened, I had uncharacteristically decided to take Moki outside at eight o'clock *and* nine o'clock for no particular reason. It happened at eight o'clock. Although a three-quarter moon shone from above, it wasn't light enough for me to see Moki's eyes. So, I missed the cue.

The teenaged puppy, Pete, the dog that Moki feared, stayed fifteen feet away. Moki had snarled and snapped at him often enough that he knew not to come any closer. But Moki still felt afraid. Cooper, Pete's dog-brother, stood five feet away. Just then, Bandit, a doggie friend of Moki's, ran up to Moki. Still afraid because of Pete's mere presence, Moki snarled at Bandit. I said, "Bad dog! That's your friend, Bandit."

Moki turned and leaped through the air at me. He began biting my heavy, winter gloves and wouldn't stop. I was too shocked and alarmed at what was happening to speak. He kept biting and I kept backing up. I kicked out at him, but I never connected, and he kept biting my gloved hands without stopping.

I felt too terrified to notice if the other dogs were around or not. After I backed up fifty feet with Moki biting me the whole time, the upstairs neighbor, Steve, whistled for his dogs. It broke the spell. I don't know if it was the whistle or the dogs' departure that stopped the attack.

Moki slunk off, still growling. I said, "Let's go inside," and started walking toward our door. He went first. The door was at the end of a long, narrow passageway. As I stepped into it, I realized that if I walked in after him, I'd corner him at the far end. Since I couldn't let that happen, I called to him to come out. He came, and I asked him to wait while I walked through the passage before him. I opened the door, walked in, and then let Moki in.

Immediately, I walked over to his kennel, opened it, and told him to go inside. He still dragged the retractable leash behind him. There was no way I could unhook it from his collar, so I closed the door on him with the leash hanging out. He kept growling the entire time.

I knew that I still needed to take him out again at nine o'clock so he could pee before we went to sleep. He calmed himself down in his kennel, and I attempted to calm myself down. At nine o'clock, I found his ball and started bouncing it and smiling. I clapped my hands and opened the kennel. Moki came bounding out, wagging his tail, and jumped at the ball. I quickly unhooked the retractable leash from his collar. That would be the last time he would have a leash on him for a week.

We walked outside, he did his business, and we walked back inside. I put him in the kennel for the night. Moki had a ritual where he came to my bed and said good-night every night and said good morning every morning. After the attack, I felt too afraid to allow him to do that.

I was scared to death of my dog, and I knew I could not get past such a vicious attack. Moki, the dog that I loved, would have to be given up. Or so I thought. Instead, we were about to experience a miracle and to embark upon a healing journey of a lifetime.

Part One:

How It All Began

A New Puppy!

It all started because I was too polite.

But I should start at the beginning, when I first moved to town. After searching through numerous roommate wanted ads, I found the ideal situation. I moved in with a young woman and her boyfriend in their spare room. They had two and a half dogs. The woman had two dachshunds, and the half was the boyfriend's pit bull who was usually not around. Those dogs supplied my doggie fix for a while, but I needed my own dog. I arranged to move into my own place so I could get a dog. After deciding on a Border Collie, I researched on the Internet to find a puppy that was not hyperactive and had no inbreeding in its background.

When I finally found a breeder with a pregnant dog who fit all the requirements, the breeder told me that she already had reservations for four males. Since my ex-husband had talked about giving up our female dog who didn't get along with other dogs, I thought I better get a male just in case. So, it was bad news that I couldn't reserve a pup from the breeder.

A week later, she emailed me to say that her dog had six males! Most of them were gray and white, though, and I wanted the traditional black and white. The main reason I didn't want gray, though, was because my "soul dog" (like soul mate) had been gray, and I didn't want the new dog to remind me of her. I was telling this to my roommate's boyfriend while I petted his charcoal gray pit bull, Diesel. Suddenly, I looked down at Diesel and said, " . . . unless he's *this* color!" The puppies were a charcoal gray, like Diesel, and I sent the breeder my deposit.

Although I preferred a black and white puppy, they were both already taken when it was my turn to choose. However, I had my eye on the gray and white puppy who had a white marking on his forehead that looked like a heart. He was my boy! Meet Moki!

Although the breeder lived several states away, she planned to travel cross-country to a dog show. We met in Wyoming so she could give me the puppy.

My Baby Puppy Child

Moki was beautiful—a fluffy little bundle of love. Since he was my new baby boy—my child—I treated him like I would treat a child. I fed him before I fed myself; I opened the door and let him out first. I was polite, and my politeness was almost Moki's death sentence. If you treat your dog like a human, he will treat you like a dog.

Treating Moki this way had immediate ramifications, but I did not realize my mistake. In feeding him first and letting him out the door first—seemingly innocent actions—I told him, in dog language, that he was the pack leader. Since this was a pack of two—him and me—this was bad news for me.

It began with behavioral problems that were so minor I don't even remember them. I just attributed them to puppyhood. When he was several months older, though, they came out as food aggression. He was the leader of the pack, and he felt that I had no business going near his food. In my politeness, *I* had made *him* leader of the pack, and now he was going to keep me in my place. That was learned with hindsight. At the time, I had no idea why he was food aggressive.

Around this time, Moki had a veterinarian appointment. When I told her about the food aggression, she said that I must stop it immediately. So I tried to stop it. I tried everything I could think of, including feeding him one kibble at a time. Nothing worked. After another vet appointment, she emphasized that I *must* get him to stop.

This was the point where I made a bad decision—listening to her. Two dogs before Moki, I had another dog that was food aggressive. Our vet back then recommended a dog behaviorist. The behaviorist said, "Why are you trying to take the food away from the dog? What would you do if someone took away *your* food? Give the dog her food!"

Writing now from the perspective of knowing why this whole thing occurred, I see that his advice wasn't exactly spot on, either. Had I considered his advice, though, the rest of this story *and* the healing it brought with it, may not have happened. Yet, it was still better advice than a blanket statement of stopping the food aggression without any understanding of why it was occurring in the first place.

The Really Bad Thing

At some point during the struggle to get Moki to stop acting food aggressive, I mentioned the problem to a friend. She related a story about a dog at obedience school and how using a choke collar had fixed the problem instantly. I had tried everything else and felt desperate to find a solution.

Next time before I fed Moki, I put the choke chain on him. Then I put his food down. When he growled as I tried to pet him, I used the choke chain. It didn't go well and scared the hell out of me. Next feeding, the same scenario, but with a different outcome. After he finished eating, Moki would not let me pet him. I realized immediately that I had done a very, very bad thing. I never did it again.

And although I only did the bad thing two brief times, it had far reaching consequences. Our whole relationship had changed in that instant. The trust was gone between us. Over the next few months, he bit me several times for no good reason—except that he felt scared—scared that I would do that bad thing to him again.

Part Two:

Happy Tail-Waggin' Times

Veterinary Woes and Wows

I eventually left the vet who told me that I *had* to fix Moki's food aggression issue. When I had Moki neutered, he was brought into the examining room for the vet to look at before they let me see him. Then the vet came out with him, handed me some prescription body salve that she said she wasn't charging me for, and told me that Moki's skin was very sensitive and I needed to put the salve on him several times a day. I thanked her for her kindness and took him home.

I was horrified the first time I put the salve on. Bright red welts covered his entire tummy where he had been shaved. But it didn't dawn on me until the following day exactly what had happened. When I had him roll over so I could put the salve on, the red welts had turned into scabs. The vet gave me the medicine for free because what happened to Moki had nothing to do with his skin being sensitive and everything to do with the clipper. Either the clipper or the person using the clipper had cut deeply into his delicate tummy skin. I found another vet immediately.

The irony was that I had just watched an episode o f *Grey's Anatomy* where the doctors had made a mistake. The hospital's board of directors cited studies that said people were less likely to sue if hospitals admitted their mistakes. I wanted to write this vet a note saying that I would never return to her. If she had said that something was wrong with the clipper or someone new had used it and accidentally hurt Moki, then I would have been compassionate and forgiving. As it was, I considered her a liar.

My new vet was awesome. She loved Border Collies and had pictures of them all over the examining room. Moki loved her and she loved him. Going to the vet had become something Moki loved to do. Once when he got a little snappy with the technicians who drew his blood, they warned the vet to use a muzzle. When she came into the examining room carrying the muzzle, Moki jumped up on her and licked her face. She held up the muzzle and said, "I guess I won't be needing this!"

The Tell-Tale Heart

The heart on Moki's forehead wasn't just for show—he meant it. He is the most loving dog I have ever had. If I sit at my desk, he has to be at my feet—touching my feet. If I sit on the couch, he is right beside me. When I'm in bed, his body always touches mine. I loved it. I'm an affectionate person, and this suited my personality perfectly. Moki was a total love.

When Moki reached his full size, hugging was his favorite affectionate pursuit. When I'd put out my arms, he would get into a semi-circle and press against me. He knew how to give a hug!

If Wishes Were Horses

When Moki was an older puppy, I volunteered at a therapeutic riding organization that provided horseback riding opportunities to help disabled children and adults. Since the owner had two dogs, all the gentle horses were used to dogs. So, before sessions started, I would walk Moki all around the corral. One horse in particular, Stevie, adopted Moki. He'd come to the fence and put his head over. I'd hold Moki up so he could sniff Stevie. When Moki was on the ground, Stevie would put his head through the fence so he and Moki could bond.

At the time, I lived in a guesthouse. The landlord's daughter had horses and often kept them in front of my little house. Ryder was an especially friendly horse. If he didn't put his head down where Moki could reach it, Moki would jump up so he could lick Ryder's nose. Then, Ryder would put his head down, and Moki would lick him so much on the nose that Ryder's normally reddish fur would take on a dark, wet look. Moki couldn't get enough of his friendship with horses. And I was all for it!

The Three Brothers

There were three brothers who used to come to the therapeutic riding center. Immediately after their session, they wanted to see Moki, who had been waiting for me in the car. The three brothers would rush over to my car. When I opened the door, Moki bounded out trying to get as much petting as he could.

All three brothers adored him, and Moki couldn't get enough of their attention. One of the boys, Bobby, would stick his face in the car, and Moki would lick and lick and lick until Bobby's face was sopping wet with dog slobber. But it didn't daunt him. Bobby kept standing there and Moki kept licking! I think the brothers liked their playtime with Moki as much as they liked riding the horses.

Sheep Around the Clock

Many years ago when I was at a country fair in Maine, I saw how amazing Border Collies could be when they worked sheep. So after I got Moki, I decided I wanted him to be a sheep dog. I looked on the Internet for the correct commands, set up some chairs in the middle of the room to be the sheep, and we started. The first commands that I taught him were "Come By"—go clockwise around the sheep—and "Away to Me"—go counterclockwise around the sheep.

The sheep—rather, the chairs—were quiet, so I didn't think it would be difficult for Moki to learn the commands. He picked up Come By and Away to Me quickly, so I threw in some hand signals to ask him to lie down. Every evening when I set up the chairs in the middle of the room, Moki got excited. I thought he was a natural.

Just when I was feeling enthusiastic about his sheepdog-ness, I attended a mini-class on herding sheep. After sitting patiently and hanging on every word in the class, they told me what I didn't want to hear. It is not good practice to work a dog on fake sheep. It had to be real sheep for the dog to become a good working sheep dog. I retired the chairs back to their corral; and that was the end of our sheep herding days.

Cat Whisperer

We lived out in the country, and along with the horses, there were small rodents. So, my landlord's daughter brought home two "barn cats." The cats lived in the barn and were untouched and untouchable. Moki and I would see them on our daily walks, but aside from a mild interest on both our parts, we left them alone.

One day when I was waiting for Moki to go to the bathroom, one cat came within fifteen feet of us and started meowing pitifully. It would meow, lie down in the dirt, roll onto its back, and then meow some more. Moki and I watched and wondered what it was doing. This occurred every day with the cat gradually getting closer and closer to us.

I had the feeling the cat wanted some attention. So, when the cat came close, I allowed Moki to walk slowly in that direction. He seemed to know he should be quiet and easy. Soon, they were sniffing noses. A few days later, as the cat's confidence grew, the cat stood on her hind legs and rubbed up against Moki's chest. Moki loved the attention, but mostly used the opportunity to sniff the cat's butt!

I couldn't touch the cat, but Moki had turned into the original Cat Whisperer! The cat loved Moki and waited for us each day to come out so it could bond with Moki. All this time, the second cat watched from afar, not wanting any part of the group entertainment. Weeks passed. Moki and the first cat had become best friends. Occasionally, I could sneak in a quick pet before the cat ran away from me.

Finally, the second cat thought maybe it was missing something after all. Slowly, slowly, it started approaching Moki. Since Moki had been friends with the first cat for so long, he wasn't as careful with the second cat. And that scared the second cat. So, it took much longer before it trusted Moki enough to rub up against him. The second cat never trusted me enough to let me pet it. But Moki had them both tamed.

Moki's friendship with the two cats amazed the landlord and his daughter. No one else could get close to either cat, but Moki had them practically eating out of his paw!

Tricks

One reason I love Border Collies is because they are so brilliant. I like teaching dogs tricks. Even old dogs. Yes, they can learn, too! But Moki was young and vibrant and eager to learn anything I had to teach. After teaching him all the normal obedience commands—sit, stay, down, heel—we moved on to my favorite trick and one that I have taught every dog I've ever had: jumping through a hoop.

It's not hard to teach. First, I'd put the bottom of the hoop on the ground and ask him to walk through it a few times. Then, I'd slowly lift it up higher and higher, and he'd jump through on his own. Moki and I both enjoyed it. I never did try it with fire, though!

Another trick that I taught him was to roll over. I'm not sure if he didn't like it, or just wanted to get it over with, but it was the fastest roll over I'd ever seen. He was back standing on his feet again before you even realized he had done it. I had to be careful where I asked him to begin because he wouldn't look at obstacles or consequences. He'd just go for it.

The square dance group that I belonged to didn't have enough men to go around, so I was always looking for a partner. After watching a video on the Internet of a Border Collie in a dance routine, I realized I could teach Moki to be my partner. He learned do-si-do quickly, but when I taught him how to alamande left, I accidentally taught him the woman's part, not the man's. Since it takes more effort to un-teach than to teach, although Moki was still enthusiastic about it, I lost interest.

Mirror, Mirror on the Wall

When Moki was very young, the sliding doors on my closet were mirrors. Moki would stand in front of them and watch my every move. I've never been sure if he realized that he was watching me. Experimenting with other mirrors when he was older, I gave him hand signals, and he always obeyed. But I didn't know whether he would obey if someone else gave him the same signal—meaning that he might think he was obeying someone other than me.

There are only a few animals that are capable of self-recognition—recognizing themselves in a mirror: they include primates, dolphins, and elephants. Dogs don't. The way Moki acts in a mirror, sometimes, I feel like he is so close. As brilliant as this dog is, it wouldn't surprise me if he were the first one to make that jump.

My Muse

Moki had many nicknames. One was Fluffy Boy because he was always so fluffy. In the morning, he would come to my bed and put his cold nose on my face to wake me up. Then, with the tip of his tongue, he would give me these tiny, little dog kisses. That was cute, but it was the cold nose that woke me up. It always made me laugh.

Since laughing was such a great way to start the day, I appreciated Moki's antics. One morning, as he backed away from me still wagging from our ritual, I knew there was a story in that morning cold nose moment. That is how my children's book called *Why Do Puppy Dogs Have Cold Noses?* was born. Fluffy Boy, my nickname for Moki, was one of the main characters.

Playing Telephone

Moki isn't just the most affectionate dog I've ever had, he is also the most talkative. It started when I was working on my computer and he wanted to play. He'd sit near me with his ball in front of him. Then, he would make an "mmm" sound. So, I would make an "mmm" sound. To which he would reply with an "mmmMMM" sound, and I would copy it back to him. The sounds between us would escalate, his tail would start wagging, and when his talking reached a sound like, "ru-ru-ru," he'd jump up and bring me the ball.

Sometime after he realized that his verbalizing succeeded in getting me to play, he tried it at other times when he just wanted attention. The game always started the same: with a single "mmm" sound. And when it escalated to the "ru-ru-ru," he'd wag his tail, jump up, and run toward me. I enjoyed the interaction so much that I always welcomed him into my arms with a big hug.

Moki doesn't just verbalize to play. He is very adept at asking for what he wants in as close as he can get to human language. Sometimes when I'm petting him, if I stop for a second to do anything else, he will make the "mmm" sound. Then, I'll pat him again and take my hand away. "Mmm" and I'll pat him again and take my hand away. He'll keep up the game as long as I'm willing to play. As soon as I say, "Enough," though, he'll stop.

Another funny thing that Moki does happens when I sneeze. I always say, "Bless you," to anyone who sneezes, even if I don't know them. A sneeze doesn't feel complete without that. If no one was around when I'd sneeze, I'd "bless" myself. Moki noticed this somehow, and now he always says "bless you" to me in his own doggie way. Usually, he'll jump up on me—the only time I allow that. But sometimes he'll just whine and give me his paw. It's like he knows I like some acknowledgement of my sneeze. He provides it.

Two Dogs in One

Moki and I had started hiking with my friend, Bill, and Dobby, his young Golden Retriever. Bill was fifteen years my senior and could out-hike me by more than fifteen times. He hiked every day, but mostly chose to hike the "fourteeners"—mountains fourteen thousand feet high. Since I had no desire to attempt a feat like that, Bill consented to hike with me on his "rest" days. His "easy" hikes wore me into the ground.

Because Bill hiked every day and had been hiking in the same area for years, we would often meet people on the trail that he knew. On our hikes, Moki and Dobby always ran loose. Whenever we met people Bill knew, I'd leash up Moki and stand to the side while Bill talked to them.

One day, we met a man that Bill hadn't seen in years. While they talked, the man petted Dobby, and Moki and I stood to the side. But they talked so long, the man got bored with petting Dobby and came over to pet Moki. I felt so frightened of what Moki might do to the man while on leash that I dropped the leash and walked a few steps away. Even back then I knew that my fear badly affected Moki. I didn't think he'd bite the man while on his own, but if he was attached to me by the leash, I thought he might. Nothing happened, and we continued our hike.

Another time Bill and Dobby took Moki and me to a wonderful loop trail that Bill had discovered along some old logging roads. It was fall, and the scenery was spectacular. It was like hiking through a tapestry of fall colors.

After a long hike uphill, we finally arrived at the top of the trail and sat on a log to eat our lunch. Moki and Dobby ran around sniffing and playing tag with each other. Whenever I talk to Moki, he always tilts his head like he is trying to understand me. This always delighted Bill, and he commented, "Moki has enough personality for two dogs!" Moki and I both smiled at that.

Bill and I spent a lot of time together hiking and talking. I discovered something during our long conversations. In the past, I knew I had some fears about possibly irrational things: mountain passes, being in a large city, and being out alone at night. It was only when confronted with several fears at once that I realized how fear-driven my life was.

For the first couple of years that I lived in the mountains, I didn't do any hiking because I feared mountain lions. When I discussed it with Bill, he said the chances of even seeing a mountain lion are remote, and they wouldn't risk attacking a person with a dog anyway. The way he put it, they don't want to take a chance on getting hurt. My fear of bears was minimal, but Bill said they wouldn't want anything to do with a dog, either.

Closer to hunting season, I told Bill that I wouldn't hike at all during that time. Bill said he would not let hunters stop him from hiking. He added that he only occasionally ran into them on the trail. With his encouragement, I bought myself a vest and an orange hat, and Bill bought Moki a bright orange vest to wear. Trouble was, I was too afraid to put the vest on Moki. I'd put the vest on his back, but before I could latch it up, I immediately felt fear—for no particular reason—which Moki would react to, and then I couldn't go any further. Honestly, though, I was glad it didn't work because it gave me an excuse not to go hiking with all those scary hunters out there.

    The truth is that I was living a fear-driven life. And most of those fears had nothing to do with Moki.

Part Three:

Two Lives Lived in Fear

Atmosphere of Fear

After that final, unsuccessful attempt at stopping Moki from growling at me when he ate, I stopped trying to correct his food aggression. I gave him his food and left him alone. But the repercussions from that carried on and on and on. At the time, I used a Gentle Leader head collar to walk him. Part of it went over his muzzle and then hooked together behind his head. I felt too afraid to put it on him. The only way I could do it was to lie on the floor while he stood above me. I felt that if I were unthreatening, then he wouldn't feel the need to threaten me. That made me feel safe. Then, I would reach up and put it on him.

Another aftereffect was that I became hypersensitive to anything he did. Moki has a little black "mustache" right beneath his nose. Suddenly, I noticed him wiggling that mustache. He may have done it every day of his life before, but until I became frightened of him, I never noticed it. So every time I saw him wiggling his mustache, I inadvertently sent out fear feelings, and Moki picked them up every time. What started as Moki just being a dog and sniffing the air (which wiggled his mustache) became a constant source of fear for me.

Such an atmosphere of fear pervaded our home that I don't know how either of us survived it. Moki slunk around the house all the time because he felt afraid of me. And because he slunk around the house, that scared me. The only time I didn't feel afraid of him was when he wagged his tail, which he rarely did because he felt so afraid. So I had to encourage him to wag his tail. If I could get him to wag, it meant he didn't feel afraid. And when he wagged, I didn't feel afraid. The situation slowly started to improve after that, but we were still afraid of each other much of the time.

Since he hadn't reached his first birthday yet, I kept him in a crate when I wasn't home. On one particular day, I knew I'd be gone longer than he could hold it, so I asked a friend to stop by and let him out for me. When my friend came over and started to open the crate, he snarled at her. The crate opened, he walked out still snarling, and then he peed on the carpet. She told him to go back into the crate and he did. That didn't work out.

A year after that happened, I had to go out of town for ten days. I asked the landlord's daughter, who Moki knew very well and liked very much, to take care of him while I was out of town. When I reached my destination and checked my voicemail, I had a message that Moki had done the same thing to her. Although not confined to the crate anymore, he snarled, peed on the carpet, and wouldn't let her close to him. I called her and told her to try clapping her hands, smiling, and saying happy things to him. It worked. Still, it was disconcerting that he acted that way with someone that he knew so well. And it only served to make my fears worse.

A year before the extreme biting event happened, my relationship with Moki had become much better. I felt much less fearful, which made Moki much less fearful. We got along great. Except for me. Whenever everything ran smoothly between us for several weeks, I would think to myself how good it felt that everything was going smoothly. Then I would become afraid that it had been so long since anything had gone wrong, that maybe it was time for something to go wrong. I'd feel the fear again and sometimes even picture him snarling at me. Whenever that would happen, Moki actually snarling at me wasn't far behind. Then he felt afraid again and I felt afraid again, and it would take days for us to feel comfortable with each other. And the cycle would start over.

Because I had petted Moki on the back to elicit a response during the brief choke chain affair, he was often sensitive about having his back touched. When he was younger and I let him sleep on the bed with me, if my foot accidentally touched him in the middle of the night—even through the covers—he would growl and sometimes snap, and then get off the bed. Later, this behavior came out if someone or something touched his back unexpectedly. So, whenever I had to swish the snow off his back during the winter, I was aware of the danger—which made me fearful—which in turn made Moki fearful and expectant of the worst. It was another symptom of our fear-driven relationship.

Another Dog Complicates Everything

Moki always got along well with other dogs. That was something I always felt confident about. Six months before the extreme biting incident, something happened to change that. After we had parked at our favorite trailhead, Moki jumped out of the car. Two dogs approached. One I recognized—she lived nearby and often appeared as we started our hikes. The other, a male, I had never seen before. When the two dogs reached Moki, I didn't realize I needed to be cautious. In an instant, the unknown male dog "attacked" Moki. Thirty seconds later, it was over, but the effects remained. Moki had never experienced an aggressive dog, and this experience changed his whole view of other dogs. Two weeks later, I realized how much.

Moki and I had just stepped out our front door. The two puppies, Pete and Oatie, now grown bigger than Moki, crowded him in our narrow passageway. The upstairs neighbor wasn't around to watch them. Moki snarled and snapped at them. At the time, I thought it was because Oatie was mostly black and resembled the dog that attacked him. Now I think it was because the two puppies had grown into clumsy teenagers who were bigger than Moki. And when they suddenly approached him in the passageway, it threatened him. Would this have happened if that other dog at the trailhead hadn't attacked him? I'll never know the answer to that question.

Shortly after the encounter in the passageway, the upstairs neighbors gave Oatie away and got another dog, Cooper, a dog they had previously owned. Moki liked Cooper, but when Cooper and Pete were together, Moki still felt threatened. In the evening when I walked Moki, if Pete and Cooper were outside, Moki always felt afraid. He would often give me this wide-eyed look of terror—even though Pete was many feet away—and I knew the look wasn't good. When I saw the look, I would immediately break the moment and ask Moki to come inside with me, while I moved us away from the dogs. Looking back, I think the extreme biting event could have happened any of these many times when Moki gave me that wide-eyed look of terror. The difference was that when I saw that look, I always did something about it—I protected him from the perceived danger. But the night of the extreme biting, it was too dark for me to see his cue.

Part Four:

The End of Life as We Knew It

Fifty Ways to Bite Your Mother

The night I took my dog outside
When past and future did collide
Another dog, a fright, surprise
I missed that fear shone in his eyes.
Attached by leash and not so free
And so he turned his fear on me.
A lunge, a bite, then many more
All from the dog I did adore.
He backed me up with great dismay
as he kept biting all the way.
For fifty feet, he lunged and bit.
My voice stayed still, I must admit.
And when I felt in great despair,
A whistle floated through the air.
The bites, they stopped without delay.
The dogs that scared him ran away.
I didn't know then just how to feel
I never thought our rift could heal.
But now our future seems so clear
For love has triumphed over fear.

Later, lying in bed and going over the terrifying events in my mind, I knew I couldn't keep Moki. How could I ever forget that initial lunge, the continued biting, and the bruises I saw on my fingers when I removed the gloves? No, I could never get over it, and thus it ended the fearful relationship between Moki and me. Or so I thought.

The irony of this is that on my Facebook page, mostly what I posted were positive affirmations and encouraging words: don't argue for your limitations; you are stronger than you think; you can do it! Here I was, arguing for my limitations, thinking myself weak, and "knowing" I couldn't get over it. Wicked irony. Sometimes we teach best what we most need to learn.

Part Five:

Aftermath

Trying to Find a New Home for Moki

The morning after the extreme biting, I clapped my hands, smiled, and let Moki out of his crate. I took him outside, fed him, and everything seemed like normal. Moki didn't realize that our whole world had shifted. I couldn't keep him. That much was clear.

Since Moki and I had troubles almost from the beginning of our time together, I knew exactly what I had to do. I would take him back to the breeder. My plan was to email her and ask for her help, then drive out there (a two-day drive), and leave him there—with or without her permission. I'd do anything to save this dog. A good friend volunteered to drive out there with us, but she thought it would be better if I called the woman and told her exactly what had happened and *ask* her to take him.

When I called the breeder, I spent twenty-five minutes on the phone, crying hysterically and begging her to take him. She kept saying she couldn't and gave me many reasons why not. And I kept telling her what a great dog he was except for this one thing, how I thought she could rehabilitate him, and how much he looked like his champion father. Until she actually said,

"No," I kept crying and begging. Once she said no, I stopped trying. Then, she suggested that I put him down.

I hung up the phone, still crying hysterically. Ironically, Moki came over to comfort me. We hugged then and hugged probably fifty times that day. I knew our time together was almost done. The thought of losing him devastated me, but the thought of keeping him terrified me. That wasn't an option.

First, I called several people in town who might know someone who could take him. One person, knowing the issues I had with Moki in the past, said I was doing the right thing. Her support made me cry even more, but didn't ease the loss of my baby. Even after the attack, he was still my baby boy.

I also called a good friend of mine who would understand my dilemma. She was a dog person, and I had even helped her pick out her first dog. Pattie was devastated by the news and felt certain that someone could fix Moki. I thought so, too, but I knew that I couldn't be the one to do it. For someone whose favorite quote is, "Don't argue for your limitations," I was sure arguing for mine. I had decided that I would wait five more days to find a home for him and then I would have to put him down. I was way too afraid to keep him. Pattie tried to talk me out of the death sentence. She wanted me to extend the date or find someone else to take him temporarily.

After talking to Pattie, I started checking the Internet for Border Collie rescues. They didn't put dogs down, and that was my first priority. He was too good a dog for that, and I knew that my fear issues created most of his problems. I either emailed the rescues or filled out forms on their websites. With every one, I made it clear that I would deliver him—no matter where they were located. I wrote to rescues all over the United States and a couple in Canada. Several replied right away that they were full or they didn't take dogs with a history of biting. I cried even more.

Then, I wrote to Frank Bell, a horse whisperer friend of mine who lives in Australia. He is American, though, and has many animal contacts in the States. Later that day, he called me to say he had a friend who might be willing to take him. I felt elated and I fell asleep that night with hope that Moki would find a good home.

The following morning, I took Moki out without a leash, because I was still too afraid to put it on him. We came out the long passageway, and our plumber was leaning inside his truck to retrieve something. Moki, my vicious dog, ignored my pleas to come back to me and ran up to the plumber.

Needless to say, I was freaking out. But his tail was wagging, so I hoped for the best. The plumber turned around, and Moki jumped up on his chest and licked him in the face. Luckily, the plumber was a dog person and after making Moki get down, he gave him a good petting. Moki returned to me all smiles like he had done a good thing.

Later that day, Frank emailed to say that his friend didn't want the dog because he already had two. But, he was going to check around. He said there was a dog whisperer somewhere who would want a challenge.

Meanwhile, more and more of the Border Collie rescues answered my requests and said no for various reasons. But Frank mentioning the dog whisperer gave me an idea. I started checking the Internet for dog whisperers. Most of what came up was the famous person on television, but interspersed were a few others. I wrote to every one of them, all over the United States, asking them to take Moki. I received answers from several of them right away, but none of the answers were what I wanted to hear. They all said they couldn't take the dog. But some of them gave me sales pitches and some offered to help. Help isn't what I needed. I needed a miracle. Moki needed a miracle. Because a miracle was the only thing that could save him. Lucky for Moki—and me—I got one.

The Miracle that Changed Everything

Right before I went to sleep, I received a response that gave me hope. She was a dog whisperer in New Jersey, named Janice. She said that she could fix the dog, but she wanted to know what I wanted her to do with him after she fixed him. Then, she asked me to call her. She was the first person who made me feel heard.

Janice runs an organization that rescues shelter dogs, rehabilitates them, trains them to be service dogs, and then gives them to autistic children. I knew Moki would be perfect for that! He would be a natural! What a great outcome! My loss would give some child a fantastic dog. Again, I felt elated when I went to sleep that night.

Next morning, instead of calling, I wrote Janice a long letter explaining in detail everything that had happened with Moki and telling her what an incredible service dog he would be. She emailed me right back asking me to call her.

I called Janice with a high expectation of sealing the deal. In my mind, I already had the car half packed to deliver him to his new home in New Jersey. Janice said no way. She could not accept a dog with a history of biting. I was devastated. It felt like this had been my final hope, and now it was gone, too. Tears poured out of me.

Although I normally have a knack for remembering exact words of conversations, those fifteen minutes were an agonizing blur. They didn't feel good at all. I remember her saying that no one would love Moki as much as I do. It made me cry harder. She said that she's normally not like this, but she felt that I needed tough love. She told me that she couldn't help me if I couldn't help myself. Finally, she said she was breathless and had to get off the phone, but I should call her that evening.

Janice, my angel, got to me. Whatever she said, worked. She had said exactly what I needed to hear. How fortuitous that I should find Janice. And how incredibly generous she was to take the time to talk me out of doing something that I could never have forgiven myself for. It wasn't just good fortune and generosity. This was a miracle. I knew it would take a miracle to save Moki, and a miracle is exactly what I received. What I didn't realize at the time was that it was a miracle for me, too.

Moki wasn't going anywhere. I would keep my baby boy. Janice would fix him, and more importantly, I would get fixed. Still, I knew I could not get over my fears by myself. After I hung up with Janice, I immediately made an appointment to see an EMDR therapist in town.

EMDR stands for Eye Movement Desensitization and Reprocessing. It is a specialized psychotherapy treatment using "sensory stimulation from a rhythmic, bilateral source" (Wikipedia). The reason I knew to go directly to EMDR was because my ex-husband, a Viet Nam veteran, used it to get over the posttraumatic stress from his terrible war experiences. It made remarkable changes in his life. And it isn't long-term therapy—usually, a few sessions resolves the problem. I knew that was the answer for me. If anything could get me over that horrible image of Moki repeatedly biting me, as well as the earlier images of the other bites, it would be EMDR.

I called Janice at the appointed time, and she said I sounded different. Of course I sounded different! I was a completely new person! My dog would stay my dog, and we would both be fixed!

Janice and I discussed getting together for Moki's "treatment," and I told her about my upcoming EMDR treatment. She wanted me to start with one of the dog whisperers in her organization, Jade, who lived in the same state as me. I really wanted Janice to do everything, since she was the one who saved Moki—and me—but she was unavailable at the time. She felt confident that Jade would do a great job for me with all the preliminary work. Then, when Janice came out later in the month to see Jade, she would come a couple days early to work with me for the final lessons.

In what felt like an instant, my life went from losing my dog, possibly having to put him down, to a wondrous new life, *with* my dog; a life filled with hope—and love. Don't forget the love.

Part Six:

The Healing

The First Day of the Rest of My Life

When I spoke to the local dog whisperer, Jade, she immediately made me feel at ease. My first job with my boy was to walk him on a leash. Since the extreme biting a few nights earlier had happened while he was *on leash*, this was not an easy task for me. The thought of attaching the leash to his collar and having him walk beside me terrified me. I was afraid he would bite my hands again. Jade said to just have the leash next to me for a while and try to move on from there.

I walked across the room, took it off the peg, and brought it over to my chair. Normally, I used the retractable leash when I took him outside, and the other leash only for when we went hiking. So, when I took the leash off the peg, Moki was immediately interested. When I laid it on the floor beside me, he laid down next to it.

Taking a deep breath, I picked up the leash and hurriedly attached it to his collar. He acted excited, and I felt scared. I took the end of the leash, stood up, and made one circle around the living room. Once was enough. Because I felt too scared to go on, I abruptly dropped the leash and sat back down. That confused

Moki. I felt too scared to take the leash off his collar. After I sat down, I waited briefly, and then asked him to bring me the ball. That always makes him happy and gets his tail up in the air. Once he wagged his tail, I felt safe and took the leash off his collar.

Later that evening when it was time for him to go outside, I decided I would try it again. I went to the door, grabbed the leash, and hurriedly put it on him. If I did it quickly, it didn't feel so scary. I walked out the door first, and he followed. I took two steps—and something welled up inside me just this side of panic. I had to turn around, come back inside, and take the leash off before I could take him outside.

Let the Healing Begin

    The following morning, I decided that I could do it. I put the leash on him, and we walked outside. Then I asked him to heel. We lived in an area that was two minutes from our hiking place, so I hadn't asked him to heel in more than a year. In a few minutes, though, he remembered what he should do and was fine.
    Later, I had time before driving to see the EMDR therapist in town, so I took him out with the leash again. It wasn't as difficult to put it on him that time. Since Jade had instructed us to take walks, I decided it was a good time to start. We got into the car, and I drove over to the hiking place. We stepped out of the car, and I felt fine. I planned to take one of our normal walks, which took twenty minutes. But we walked only a few minutes down the road when I pictured him biting my hands, so we had to return.
    I had to honor my fears at that point. Since I had pushed myself so hard to get there, I felt it was far enough. Tomorrow would be another day, and hopefully we could go farther.
    I drove to town, parked my car, and followed my new therapist's directions to his office. Ryan, my

therapist, left some paperwork outside the office for me to fill out. Promptly at my appointed time, he came out with a smile. I liked him already. For those who have never had a therapist, it is important to like him (or her) and to have a connection. Otherwise, you will not progress as fast.

His office was warm and bright, with a gas fireplace that made the room homey. I felt comfortable. Our first session consisted of general preliminary questions: where I grew up, my relationship with my parents, my relationship with my siblings, etc. When we set up the appointment, I had told him about the incident that provoked my wanting EMDR. When I asked how many sessions it would take, he said it depended on the "feeder issues." During the two days before my appointment, I made a list of all the fears I could think of, and my friends added some that I hadn't thought of which I reluctantly wrote down.

Toward the end of our time, Ryan said that he thought we could begin the EMDR immediately in the following session. "Sometimes the EMDR provokes intense feelings of the painful emotion. But you are stable enough and have enough of a support network to get right to work. Our next session should be an hour and a half."

I replied, "Besides this one gigantic issue, I feel like I have my life together!" He laughed, we shook hands, and he said that he enjoyed meeting me. I told him I liked him, too.

Doing My Own Healing

That evening, I started my own healing work with EFT and the Healing Codes. EFT stands for Emotional Freedom Technique. It is something I have used off and on for years. Using your fingers, you tap on certain acupuncture meridian points. First, you decide on a "set-up" statement. I used "Even though Moki bit me, I deeply and completely accept myself." As I said this several times, I tapped on a certain place on my hand. Then, I tapped on the other specific meridian points while I said, "Moki bit me." If you still feel the issue is "hot," then you come up with another set-up statement, such as, "Even though I'm afraid of Moki, I deeply and completely accept myself." You use your intuition depending on what comes to mind next. Sometimes it's as slight a change as, "Even though I'm still afraid of Moki, I deeply and completely accept myself."

The Healing Codes are based on the work of Alexander Loyd and his book, *The Healing Code*. According to Dr. Loyd, the Healing Code system can correct any physical or emotional issue. So I followed the directions and did several minutes of that, as well. When I finished, I felt "funny." What exactly funny meant, I can't say, but it was different—as if something was going on inside me. It went away after a while. I decided that I would continue with my EFT and Healing Code "treatment" several times a day until my next therapy session, which would be the first EMDR treatment. Although I couldn't tell for sure, it felt as if the Healing Codes had taken the "edge" off my fear. Time would tell.

Unstable Energy

Jade sent me some documentation. Some of it hit home. "Fear is unstable energy and dogs don't trust and won't follow unstable energy." I knew that my energy had been unstable and fearful since that first bite so many years ago. No wonder we had problems! Of course, I knew all along that Moki's main issue was me.

The documentation also talked about how the energy of one of us affects the energy of the other. I always knew that my energy affected him, and that I was the one who needed to change. His energy mirrored mine. If I was afraid of him—and I was—then he was also afraid of me. What a way to live. Yet, we did live that way for most of four years.

And this is true of humans, also. If you don't like someone's behavior, the only one you can change is yourself. The change in your energy will either provoke the other person to change or perhaps provoke him or her to leave, but your own energy is the only thing you can change.

I knew that Moki had fear-motivated aggression because he had fear issues of his own—probably reflected from me. But another part of Jade's documentation talked about redirected aggression: if a dog is aroused into an aggressive response by a person or animal that he is prevented from attacking or running away from, he may redirect this aggression onto someone else. That was exactly what happened to us the night of the extreme biting. He was afraid of the other dog and couldn't run or fight because he was on leash, so he redirected it onto me.

After reading the documentation, I had a long conversation with Jade. We went over many different aspects of Moki's healing. Jade wanted to start the "whispering" work with Moki right away, but I didn't feel I was ready yet. My fear levels were still very high, which limited what I could do comfortably with Moki. We had to wait.

She talked again about the importance of walking him on a leash. He needed to learn to walk next to me or behind me. The important item here was that he needed to learn to follow—to be a follower. Moki had to recognize me as the leader of the pack—not in a dominant way—but in a teaching way, a guiding way. And we must walk every day to instill the lesson in him.

She suggested getting a doggie backpack and putting in a bag of rice—anything—to make him think he has a job to do. She said with her dog it made a world of difference. Unfortunately, I told her I felt too afraid to put it on him. It shouldn't be a problem later, though.

We talked about the unstable energy—my unstable energy—and I realized how I had affected our relationship in the past with my fear. When talking about the original incident that caused the subsequent problems, she said that dogs live in the moment and do not hold grudges. Moki and I needed to relearn how to respect each other. He had to see me as the one who would provide for him and protect him. Jade said that what happened between us originally caused a gap in our communication. To begin to repair that, I had to take him out every day and keep him safe.

Since other dogs had triggered his recent biting, I asked her about that. She said that I needed to show him that I could take care of it. His immediate responses are either to fight or to run away. She said that at this point, the best solution was to avoid the situation.

I didn't know how I would do that at home, since several people let their dogs run loose around where I lived, including the big puppy that triggered his fear. But if I met someone on the trail, I should say, "We're in training." Jade said that most people would respect that. Since I had not had my EMDR session yet and my fear was still flying high, I asked if I could drop the leash if something happened and I couldn't handle my own fear. She said it would be okay if that was the only choice. It would be easier to avoid the situation than to focus my energy on it.

Jade asked me why I have a dog. Because what other creature on earth gives us more unconditional love than a dog? And who among us could refuse wonderful, glorious, unconditional love? Jade said that unconditional love depends on my ability to protect and provide for him.

Every step that I took helped to rebuild the gulf between us. And everything that I was now doing would build trust and respect. That was the key to healing for both Moki and me. Jade said that he had already forgiven me for the incident so many years ago that started this whole nightmare. But that incident broke the connection between us and damaged our trust and respect for each other. By following the correct course of action, we could build it up again and the connection between us would be even stronger.

Before we got off the phone, Jade mentioned how important walking was and that we were really moving forward. She suggested I start using the Gentle Leader collar, but I told her that I didn't have the nerve yet to put it on. I always used to use a Gentle Leader when we walked, but hadn't used it since we started hiking instead of walking. It is a wonderful device that goes over the dog's nose and mouth. And I remembered too well that Moki's mouth was full of sharp teeth. I wasn't ready yet to get so close.

Jade said that it was important while we walked that Moki stay next to me or behind me, but not in front of me. She said that I should throw my shoulders back and my chest out and act confidently. This was excellent advice.

Setting the dog issues aside, acting confident is good advice for everyone. Act confident and you'll become confident. Act happy and you'll become happy. If you walk down the street acting confident, people will notice that and treat you as if you have confidence. As people treat you like you have confidence, your confidence will increase. Soon, you will not be "acting confident" anymore, you will be confident.

So Jade had given me excellent advice. The question was, did I have the ability, the wherewithal, to follow it? Jade said that Moki and I both deserved to be whole, to be fixed. And I was confident that we were on the path that would heal us. When the journey was over, we would both be better for it.

Slow Progress

I finally felt as if we were making progress. We drove back to the hiking place and walked to the corner. It went fine until we were on our way back to the car. I felt trepidation about the possibility of other dogs being in the parking lot. There weren't any, and we drove home. Later that afternoon we returned to the hiking place and did it all again. On the way back to the car, I felt the fear again, but no one was there.

Each time when we got home, following Jade's instructions, I made sure I had already eaten, waited awhile, and then fed Moki. You go out walking to get food, and then you come home to eat. It was my duty to provide for him. This was part of the process of building trust and respect.

Two Steps Back

You know how they say one step forward and two steps back? This was a two steps back day. I drove over to the hiking place and saw that Bill, my hiking friend, and his dog, Dobby, were out of their car. I left Moki in my car and walked over to talk to Bill. When I told him that I couldn't have Moki around any other dogs right now, he went on and on about how stupid that was. He continued by questioning the credentials of my dog whisperer. Although I tried to explain that she had only suggested avoiding that situation *after* I told her that I was afraid of what might happen around other dogs, Bill still didn't listen. He walked off in a huff.

Since his dog was loose and another loose dog was coming down the road, I chose to walk the other direction. The conversation with Bill had unnerved me. Since I had just come through a major trauma and crisis, I was in no condition to feel confident. Anyone doubting my choices sent me spinning off into space. Without mincing words, I was a mess.

Moki and I managed to finish the walk, and we drove home. After I sat down at the computer, Moki came over and gave me *a look.* It was not the bad look like he used to get around that exuberant puppy, but this was a look that I recognized very well. Moki knew—he could feel—that I was a mess. He *always* gave me this look when I had unstable energy. What a revelation!

In the old days, shortly after I did the bad thing to him, he used to look at me like that all the time. At first, I'd try to pet him to make him feel better, but he'd always snap at me. Finally, I realized that petting him wasn't a good idea when he looked like that. But I never realized that he looked at me like that because *my* energy was unstable. He was a service dog—telling me that I needed to settle down!

After the conversation with Bill, and then Moki pointing out that my energy was off, I did some meditation and worked awhile on EFT and Healing Codes. It made me feel better—still not good—but better. When it came time for our evening walk, there were several cars in the parking lot at the hiking place. The other end of the parking area was a half block away, so I parked there and walked toward the regular parking lot. Moki was so excited about going toward the parking lot that he wouldn't heel. And I was still so off because of the earlier conversation with Bill that it made me feel afraid. We walked a few times back and forth, but I was still too unnerved and too upset to continue. The whole episode frightened me, and I didn't like the feeling. After a few minutes, we drove home.

What this showed me was how fragile I was. Although I had been doing the EFT and Healing Codes, I had just started and I was far from healed. I was supposed to rate the issue from one—almost nothing—to ten—terrible. So I rated the biting incident as a bursting-at-the-seams ten. After several days, I felt that I had it down to a doable eight. But eight was still very high. I had a long, long way to go. And my first EMDR treatment was not for five more days.

Look Ma, No Gloves!

In the morning, I got up extra early since it was the weekend, and we drove to the hiking place before anyone else arrived. We walked down to the corner again, while I sang the confidence song from *The Sound of Music*. On the way back to the car, I was a little wary of loose dogs. Luckily, there weren't any.

Later in the afternoon after returning from an errand, as I parked the car I noticed there were no dogs running loose outside. So I came into the house, hooked Moki to his leash, and took him outside. Note: I did not wear my heavy winter gloves! Huge progress. Thankfully, it was still winter so I didn't look like a fool when I did wear the gloves. Since he bit me, though, I hadn't had the nerve to walk him without them. This was my first glove-free walk. Although I had to admit that he peed twelve feet outside my door. So it wasn't as huge a progress as it could have been, but at least I did it. That was a start.

At five o'clock, when I had planned to take him for another walk, I heard the upstairs neighbors outside calling their dogs. So I didn't dare go out. When I heard them go in, I waited a few more minutes and then went out myself to assess the situation. No dogs, but just to make sure and to satisfy myself, I pulled my car out of its parking place and then backed in. Then, I opened the back door. If the dogs suddenly appeared, I had an out.

Returning to the house, I put Moki's leash on, and we went outside. No dogs in sight, so Moki jumped into the backseat with no problem. Instead of going to the hiking place, which was probably busy, I drove up the road to a little rest area used for putting on chains in the winter. After parking the car, I took Moki out and we began walking up and down the parking area. But it was right at the side of a busy highway, and the cars racing by agitated Moki, which in turn, scared me.

When Moki was an older puppy, we lived next to another highway. We walked along it every day, and Moki showed a propensity to want to chase cars. To try and stop that inclination, I taught him to lie down every time a car passed by.

While we walked in the rest area, at one point he was so agitated that he lay down by himself. The cars disturbed me, too, and Moki's agitation bothered me, so we walked back to the car and left. The dogs still weren't out when we arrived home, so we got into the house safely.

Jade called me that night to check on my progress. Since it had been constantly in my thoughts, I asked her what to do if the other dogs—especially Pete, the dog that triggered his behavior—are outside when I take Moki out. She said that I had to step between them and assert myself. I had to correct the other dog and send it away. She said to step forward and claim the area that we are in. Then, we turn around and go back into the house.

Jade said that I need to have a conversation with the people upstairs. She said that I should make it from the dogs' point of view so the neighbors would understand it. I should say that dogs are pack animals and that Moki would really like to be around other dogs.

And when he gets over this, he will love to play with Pete, the dog who scares him. I should emphasize how wonderful it could be if they could all play together. But if their two dogs are out there without supervision, then it is inhibiting and possibly detracting from my progress with Moki.

Jade's instruction of what to do if the other dogs appeared sounded logical—I would be showing Moki that I could protect him—but I wasn't sure if I could do it. We would be in the exact situation that caused him to bite me before. And since I am an introvert, talking to the neighbors would be as hard for me as standing up to the dogs. But I hoped that the EMDR would help me in that respect, too.

I also asked Jade about a couple different behaviors that I had noticed. One, Moki was wagging his tail more. And two, when I scratched his tummy a couple nights earlier, for the first time I could ever remember, he opened his hind legs so I could scratch him. Before, he would lie on his side and reluctantly allow me to scratch his tummy, but he would not open his hind legs. Jade said this was a sign that we were building trust. He was starting to trust me enough to be vulnerable. She said that every little step was progress.

Risk and Fear

Although it was a weekday, we got up early to go to the hiking place before Bill or anyone else arrived. We walked much farther than any of our previous walks. All went well, thankfully. Every tiny amount of progress that we made gave us more confidence—confidence in ourselves and confidence in each other.

Since Jade told me to have a conversation with the people upstairs, that was on my mind. I went outside with the intention to talk to them. When I saw their truck warming up, though, I knew they planned on leaving. I didn't want to get in the way or rush through our conversation.

Moki wanted to go outside after the truck left, but I still heard people walking around on the deck. If they were outside, there was a good chance their dogs were out with them. Before I put him on leash, I went out to check. If someone was home, there was always that chance that he or she would let the dogs out after I checked and before I put the leash on Moki. So, although the dogs were not out when I checked—I still felt scared.

I leashed Moki, and we walked outside. No one was out there, and we came back into the house with no incident. But I felt agitated. After working on EFT and the Healing Codes the previous night, I felt like I had my fear down to a seven. And when we returned from the walk, although nothing had happened, the *risk* of something happening bothered me. I couldn't sit at my desk and do my work. I needed to sit in front of the fire and calm myself down. This was no way to live; I knew I must have a conversation with the neighbors.

Talking to the Neighbors

The truck returned, I finished lunch, and it was time to step up and face this fear. I knocked on the door and Hildy answered right away. When I said I'd like to talk to her for a few minutes, she invited me in. I told her the details of the whole story and asked if she could keep the dogs in unless they were supervised. She understood completely and agreed with no hesitation. We had a nice talk, and she shared some challenges that she had with her own dogs.

Then, she told me a story of something that happened a few days before. She was out with her dogs, but she deliberately walked to the condominium down the road to keep her dogs away from our apartment. Another dog was running around with his owner, Ken. Hildy said that she heard me with Moki and remarked to Ken that she had never heard me so firm and assertive with Moki. Ken said that he hadn't, either.

That was because I was always afraid that Moki might try to bite someone. And I was unsure how to handle being around other people. That was my fear, not his. He had never attempted to bite anyone other than me. The few times that he snapped at someone was in a different context—not outside when I was around, when someone just wanted to pet him. I never realized how much my fear of him allowed him to be the leader.

After telling Jade the night before how Moki let me pet his stomach, I realized it was a few days ago and I hadn't tried it again since the disconcerting conversation with Bill. So I tried again. He didn't want his stomach scratched at all.

My energy—my composure—had not been the same since then. And although my conversation with Hildy went well, I still hadn't recovered myself from that, either. Again the reminder of how fragile I was. Moki and I both had a long way to go. But we had both come a little way and that was without the help from the EMDR or seeing the dog whisperer yet, so I felt okay with it. We were taking baby steps and that was fine with me. I may have felt fragile, but even with the fear and agitation, I also felt strong enough to continue.

Feeling Bad and Feeling Encouraged

I had another unsettled day and didn't know why. But I noticed that little things that would normally not bother me had been eating at me. I knew my energy was unstable. Moki hadn't given me the "unstable energy alert look," so I thought I was managing to keep it down to some degree. It still frustrated me. At first, I felt happy with the progress we had made, and then I felt like it stopped or even went backwards. I wanted to think that this was normal after the trauma that I had experienced—the trauma of Moki biting me, and me thinking that I had to give him up. Because, believe me, the thought of giving him up was as traumatic as him biting me. It was devastating. For three days, I cried almost every minute until Janice answered my email. Janice, my angel.

I emailed Jade to tell her of my backsliding. She had a different take on it than I did. She said that talking to the neighbors was a big step. Even if Moki didn't realize it, talking to them made me a pack leader—part of protecting and providing for Moki. She said that's what's important. And the best comment of all was when she said that I had almost made it to my EMDR appointment without any major incident! Hallelujah! I didn't realize that was such a big deal, but when I read it in her email—it made sense. I wasn't as bad off as I thought I was. I felt grateful for Jade and her support. Just having her say those encouraging words made me feel better and made my energy more stable! Although I thought I was trying to feel better, really I had just been feeling sorry for myself.

Still the Fear

As Moki and I were coming back from a quick morning walk, I saw the upstairs dogs. My heart gave a lurch, and I felt a jolt of fear before I realized they were inside the fence. Hopefully, there would come a time when seeing them didn't bother me like that.

We went on our longer morning walk early again to insure not running into anyone. There were two cars in the parking lot, so I didn't know if I might run into dogs around the next corner. I knew I'd feel grateful when my fear was gone and when Moki was no longer afraid of other dogs. Toward the end of the day, we took our evening walk. It was almost always abbreviated, because I usually felt unsure at that time.

I tried rubbing Moki's tummy again, and he let me, but I became scared and had to stop. That was something that had happened with him and me for years. When everything was going really well, I suddenly seized up and felt afraid of something bad happening. What a waste of all the love between us. I felt good that finally we could heal all this and we could both move forward. Together.

My First EMDR Appointment

Finally, the day for my first EMDR appointment arrived! I felt apprehensive and excited. When I went in to the office, first I told Ryan the details of Moki biting me and how the fears all began several years ago. Then, we started the EMDR.

First, he had me think of a place where I felt safe. I lived near Mesa Verde National Park. One of the cliff dwellings had a kiva that was accessible to the public. You climb down a ladder to enter, and then the inside is mostly original. I always loved that place—always felt safe and at home there. Even when it was busy, I sat against the wall cross-legged and enjoyed the feeling of being there. So I chose the kiva as my safe place.

Before my appointment, I had decided that I wanted him to use the eye movement rather than the earphone tones or the hand vibrations. That's where we started. While Ryan rapidly moved his fingers back and forth in front of my eyes, I visualized feeling safe in the kiva.

Ryan said it would help if I would practice going to my safe place at random times—like when I drove my car. He said if I practice, then at a moment of crisis, the safe place could kick in by itself to help me.

Next, we started on my main issue: Moki biting me. My instructions were to visualize him biting me, feel the bad feeling in my heart/solar plexus area (because that's where I felt that bad feeling), think of the words, "I am cruel and fearful," and watch and move my eyes in response to his fingers. I couldn't do it. I have ADD—attention deficit disorder. It wasn't an excuse; it was a fact. And I don't feel victimized by it, I feel blessed by it. It has given me the creativity to create my books. Even if I could have given it back, I wouldn't have. But it did have its limitations. I couldn't focus on all those things at once.

When I told Ryan about my ADD, he suggested trying the headphones with the tone and/or the hand vibrators. It did seem easier, but holding four thoughts at once was difficult for me. Each time the tones and vibrations went on for several seconds while I focused on what Ryan told me to. It seemed we were progressing. The visualization went from Moki biting me to Moki licking my face and hugging me. But the issue still felt "hot." After some discussion, Ryan said there had to be a different core issue that was causing this one to remain hot. Well, I already knew that. I had lived my life in a fearful way before Moki ever came into the picture. Now, my job was to figure that out. It was the key to our future: my future, Moki's future, and our future together.

Something came out in the session after I told Ryan how I felt about my run-in with Bill a few days earlier. It was the same feeling as when my mother was in the nursing home and my brothers questioned my judgment. I suspected that it had to do with my longtime self-esteem issues that I thought were mostly healed. But at the time, feeling so vulnerable, those past issues were closer to the surface. Bill questioning my judgment just triggered them.

Before I left his office, Ryan told me that I might have weird dreams. If I did, I should write them down. That night, a dream woke me up, and I dutifully wrote it down. When I went back to bed, I couldn't sleep because other possibilities of what caused my fears kept occurring to me. I got up again and wrote them down. I would have to discuss them with Ryan during my next appointment.

The Grip of Fear

I finally felt real progress. Before we walked in the morning, I put the Gentle Leader on that Jade had been wanting me to use. Although it was scary, I got through it, and Moki was fine. For the first time on our usual walk, Moki had his tail up in a tight spiral for almost half the walk. It might sound small, but knowing Moki and knowing how he usually held his tail, I felt this was good progress. Then we heard a nearby dog barking, and it threw us both off. After we walked away from the dog, Moki's tail was still at half-mast—not really up, but not down, either.

After we arrived home, Moki came over to me, lay down, and let me scratch his tummy. This time I didn't hesitate; I scratched his tummy, and we both liked it! More progress. Life was good.

I had been doing something wrong with Moki, and he told me about it. Moki loved salad. When I made a salad, I gave him a cucumber here, a carrot there, and some of everything that he liked. When I handed him the cucumber and the carrot, he looked at me funny. As I continued making the salad, I realized that I was allowing him to eat before me. That was a huge no-no.

That was how this whole predicament started. For the rest of the salad preparation, I set aside the vegetables that he liked, and I gave them to him after I finished eating.

Realizing that I had made this mistake—and that Moki himself had to point it out to me—scared me. Again proving how fragile I was during this process. I felt that I had given Moki mixed signals that confused him. I wasn't sure if he still considered me the pack leader—which was essential to our success.

Later, when we took our afternoon walk, I wasn't as confident as I had been—not that I had ever been overly confident in this process, but I felt even less confident. When I saw that he had his tail up as we walked, it made me feel better. I hoped that having him heel during our walk put us back on the right track.

When I took him out for a quick walk after he finished his dinner, I slipped up again. It was snowing. As much as I loved the snow, when we came into the mudroom I needed to get the snow off him before we stepped into the house. That had always scared me. He never tried to bite me when I did it, and yet I was always afraid that he would. As I brushed the snow off his back, I felt the fear, very strongly. It made me feel bad that I hadn't lost the fear yet.

After that, I felt unstable energy for hours—gratefully not bad enough for Moki to give me his alert—but unstable enough that it made me uncomfortable around him. I knew that the happier you are, the happier you are. And the worse you feel, the worse you feel. So I had to find a way to stop the bad feelings. I tried my kiva safe place. It worked. Moki came wagging to me with his ball and other toys. We played and everything felt better. When it came time to take him outside, I put the Gentle Leader on him without even a twinge of fear. Taking it off was another matter, but even putting it on without a twinge was progress. Baby steps. I had to feel satisfied with baby steps. At least we were moving in the right direction.

Surprise on the Stairs

Although Moki didn't like it, putting the Gentle Leader on did not trigger my fear response. And once it was close to his nose, he was okay with it.

It had snowed the night before, so as we walked we were in ankle deep snow in freezing weather. My fingers were cold and I didn't want to go too far. We walked to the corner and I turned around. Moki loved being out there so much that when I turned him around he usually stood for a minute and had a look on his face that said, "I don't want to turn around." That had been sending a bolt of fear through me. But this time, nothing, not even a twinge. Baby steps.

The hiking area was filled with cars and loose dogs when we went for our afternoon walk. So we drove back to the rest area at the side of the road. As we walked, Moki didn't seem anxious about the cars. He just acted like he wanted to chase them like when he was much younger. So every time a car came by, I asked him to lie down. Remembering his old training, he responded immediately. Unfortunately, traffic was heavy, so he was lying down more than we were walking! We made one trip up and back and drove home.

During the afternoon, I tried scratching his stomach again. He let me reluctantly. I tried again later. Sometimes he let me and sometimes he didn't. It might have been my energy, though I wasn't sure. As time went by, I thought he would be more willing to let me do it, and I would be more comfortable doing it.

We had a surprise when I took him out in the evening. I heard someone walking up on the deck, but I thought it was the upstairs neighbors. Since the motion light was on the other side of the stairs, I had to go over there to get it to stay on so I could see. As I stepped away from the stairs, I saw a stranger coming down. A small dog ran down the stairs in front of her. The dog came out of nowhere, and it took a minute for me to gather my wits, but I dutifully stepped between the dog and Moki, protecting him. Instead of speaking to the person, I spoke to the dog to keep him away, but finally she picked him up and took him away. Just before she picked him up, Moki strained at the leash to get to him. His tail was wagging. Although the little dog was not the dog that triggered Moki, it was huge progress on my part to step between them without thought of the possible consequences—Moki biting my butt!

A Video Bite

The morning's walk was cold again with a low windchill. But I made it to the corner before turning around. I didn't even look at Moki this time—I made the turn and pulled gently on the leash to encourage him to come with me. If he did his "I don't want to turn around" act, I didn't acknowledge it, I just kept walking. He followed.

Later in the day, I wanted to scratch Moki's stomach, and he wouldn't let me. Putting everything together, it made me realize that our healing path was not a linear journey. There would be steps forward, and there would be steps backward. And Moki and I would not necessarily be stepping forward or backward at the same time. It would be nice if we were, though!

The previous night I did something else that wasn't the brightest move on my part. A friend wanted me to watch the television dog whisperer. Although I chose a video that sounded like it would apply to my situation, it applied a little too closely. The dog bit the whisperer repeatedly. Even with living a fear-driven life, nothing on television had ever scared me before. But when I saw that dog biting him like that, it brought back all the terror of the night it happened to me. I couldn't control my fear. It made me afraid to even pet Moki. I knew I would get over it, eventually. But at the time, it felt like I had lost all the forward momentum I had gained. There I was—as scared of Moki as ever.

During the day, the vision of the biting on the video and my memory of the extreme biting began fading. By the end of the day, though, I still felt like I had lost ground. What helped me when I felt fearful was going to my kiva safe place. At such a fragile time in my life, I realized I had to be more careful.

One thought I had was that the biting wouldn't happen again, because I didn't need it to happen again. I had made all this progress in several areas of my life. If that's what the biting was about, then it had served its purpose.

Trip to See the Dog Whisperer in Boulder

A brand new day, and I felt as if I had put the fears of yesterday behind me. After a brief walk, we returned home and prepared to leave. I fed Moki, packed the car, and took off to meet Jade, Janice's dog whisperer in Colorado. She would give me the preliminary session while we waited for Janice to come to town.

We had a long drive. Moki had never been in the car so long, except when he was a baby puppy and I picked him up in Wyoming. He started crying when we were almost to the motel. Although we had stopped on the way several times, he wasn't used to being cramped in the backseat for so long.

When we arrived at the motel, we took a walk on the bike path behind it. On our way back, I saw a guy coming down the path with three dogs on leash, so I moved Moki over to the side to let them pass. The guy thanked me, chitchatted for a minute, and then said, "Well, these two can say hello." Then he dropped the leashes of two of the dogs. They ran over to Moki, and I had no time to get between them. I kept saying to the man, "Get them! Get them! Get them!" and he got them and apologized. Either Moki didn't react at all, or I didn't have time to notice. It wasn't until we were walking back to the room that I realized that I didn't have my heavy gloves on.

Boulder Behavior Lessons

It occurred to me, even before meeting Jade, how much my relationship with Moki had already shifted. I felt we had a better relationship than at any other time in the previous four years—probably since he first became food aggressive because of my politeness.

Since I had been watching the parking lot for Jade, I saw her when she parked. I watched as she approached my motel room. When she got close enough, I opened the door and let Moki out. I knew if she knocked on the door, he could be protective. But if she was outside, he would run and greet her, which he did. When he tried jumping on her, she immediately gave the "sshhh" sound. That was the same sound I learned from the horse whisperer to make horses behave.

Jade and I hugged each other and said how happy we were to meet. Oh, how I had waited for that day. Up to that point, I had to evaluate Moki's and my progress for myself. Finally, I would have someone else's opinion of how we were doing, both separately and together. And it was someone in "authority" who I trusted. I did feel reasonably confident that we were doing well. But there was always that niggling doubt that it wouldn't work out.

Jade was in her early twenties, pretty, with long hair, and an easygoing personality that immediately put me at ease. Besides being a dog whisperer, she worked at a (legal) marijuana dispensary. That cracked me up!

After she arrived, we leashed Moki and took him downstairs to walk. Jade held the leash while I walked a couple steps in front. She walked briskly, with her head up and her chest out. She said it was important that we give every air of confidence. The trail we walked had people walking or biking by. Whenever someone came by and Moki got distracted, Jade gave him a quick "sshhh" sound and a light correction with the leash. The light correction was a matter of slightly moving her fingers—not a heavy jerk of the hand. There should always be "connection" between you and the dog, so if a correction is necessary, a small motion with your fingers is enough. Since Moki is smart, he caught on quickly.

As we walked the trail with Moki between us, I had the arm closest to him drawn up to my chest. Why? Because my fears still controlled me. I was afraid he would bite my hand. I hoped I could get to the root of my fears soon, because they had become very annoying!

After a short walk, we returned to the room to discuss some of the basics. Jade and I sat across from each other, and Moki took up a place beside me, leaning against me. Jade said that if he comes over asking me to pet him, that makes him more dominant. She said I need to correct him with a "sshhh" and a gentle pull on the leash. Then, don't look at him, wait ten seconds to see if he obeys, and if not, correct again. He stopped immediately. It felt like he knew something was changing. Although he would try to push it, once I drew the line, he willingly obeyed. She said we needed to work on being comfortable together again. It would help if I kept a leash on him that was attached to my belt all the time. He would have to follow me everywhere, and he would get the idea faster that way.

About walking, Jade said it was important for both of us to have a purpose. Having a purpose would help to keep the energy down. My purpose was to walk to a safe place. Moki's purpose was to follow me. Jade suggested that if he carried a backpack, it would give him a greater sense of purpose. I felt I was almost ready to try to put one on him.

Jade talked about how much confidence her miniature pinscher had. She said he weighed only ten pounds, but he walked around like he was king. He would stand up to any dog, no matter how big. She said that watching him with so much confidence gave her confidence. If *he* could do that, then she could, too.

Once Moki and I built more trust and respect for each other, Jade said, Moki would feel confident that I would take care of him. Once that happened, everything would be easier between us. All he wanted was for me to be happy and safe.

It was important for me to have calm energy before a walk. Jade suggested that when I put the Gentle Leader on him, I should stand at his side instead of right in front of him. A Gentle Leader controls his head, much as a bridle on a horse.

Jade said that dogs live in the moment, purely in the moment. There are no grudges between dogs in a pack. Corrections are made, accepted, and everyone moves on.

We took another walk later, and I held the leash. I tried to remember everything Jade told me. I asked, "Jade, when I correct him, do I need to make the 'sshhh' sound *and* a gentle tug on the leash, or is one of those enough?"

She said, "It would be better with both, but one will do." The reason I asked was because I often remembered to do one, but not both. It was a huge learning process for me. Moki needed to learn to be a new dog, and I needed to learn to be a new person. We were both doing well so far.

After walking around some more, we came back to the room to talk. Moki lay on the floor between us. At one point, Jade gently rubbed Moki's foot with her shoe. I expected him to react to that, and he did. He made a low growl, walked away, and looked suspiciously back. Jade said the more trust that Moki and I develop between us, the more he would trust other people. That was good, because I was always leery with him around strangers.

Before Jade left, I asked her straight out, "Can Moki be fixed? Can I be fixed?"

She said, "Both of you can definitely be fixed!" Phew. I needed to hear that. She said she could see Moki and me sometime in the future going to schools and nursing homes. Wow! I liked that image!

Jade told me that when she had first talked to me and I told her that I was too afraid to put the leash on him, she thought she might need to drive down right away to take care of it. So, all the progress that we had made impressed her.

I said, "I still feel really bad about the bad thing I did with the choke chain on Moki that caused all the problems."

She said, "If that was the only mistake you made, then you're way ahead of me. You need to forgive yourself." I already knew that. It was the doing it that was hard.

I also talked about how fear driven I'd been my whole life and how all that fear led up to the situation between Moki and me. And that the extreme biting incident was just the pinnacle of all my fear. Jade said that Moki was my mirror. Whoa. That was a revelation—and it made perfect sense.

As Jade walked out the door, she said, "I needed this." She had been going through a bad breakup, and the distraction of helping me through my issues, helped her. We helped each other. What could be better than that?

Scaredy-cat

During my session with Jade the previous day, my fear issues came out several times—mostly anytime she had direct contact with Moki. I was still afraid of Moki around other people. When I thought about it later, I forgot that I had only gotten four hours' sleep the previous night. My fears always felt worse when I was sleep deprived.

On our drive home, I listened to a radio program with two disc jockeys talking to each other. Something came up about bucket lists, and the young woman said she didn't have anything on hers. The older man said that she would when she got older. She said that she didn't want anything on hers. Continuing, she said she didn't want to go to Europe because she was afraid of flying. She didn't want to go zip lining because seven years ago, a woman zip lined, got a cut, and got infected with flesh eating bacteria that ate her arm off. Everything the other guy suggested, she had fears about. It sounded overwhelmingly ridiculous. However, when I heard it, my first thought was, oh, no, is this me?

We drove home from Boulder, and as soon as we stepped into the house, I started feeling fearful again.

Moki gave me absolutely no reason to feel like that. The fear came completely from me. I knew I needed to get that fixed. My fear didn't add to his bad behavior—it caused it.

Great EMDR Session

I awoke before the alarm rang and had time to think. Jade had told me to keep the leash on Moki while he's in the house and attach it to my belt so he had to always follow me around. I didn't realize it at the time, but that scared me. During the beginning of our talks a couple weeks earlier, Jade said to me, "The good thing about the leash is that you two are attached together. The bad thing about the leash is that you two are attached together." She must have said that in response to me being afraid to put the leash on him in the beginning. But even after two weeks, I couldn't see myself attached to him. The thought of it scared me.

My second EMDR appointment turned out awesome! At the end of my previous appointment, Ryan said I might have weird dreams, and he asked me to remember them so we could discuss them. The dream I had was that someone came into my room to my bed. I woke up extremely frightened. I told Ryan about the dream and said that if the whole thing turned out to be that I was molested when I was a child (unknowingly) that it would be such a cliché that I couldn't stand it. Ryan said that he wasn't assuming anything. He would not dig for that but would wait and see where my brain wanted to go as we did the EMDR.

Ryan said he usually deals with fears that are irrational, but mine were grounded in truth. Moki *did* the extreme biting to me. I was afraid of that. That was real. He said he thought that I needed to come up with a plan in case it happened again—a plan that would make me feel safe. That was my homework.

First, he said he had thought about it and that he wanted to try something different this time. He said that he wanted me to give him a detailed play-by-play of the extreme biting incident, starting from what happened during the day to the end of the day. Ryan said the brain stores those memories differently from how it stores just the incident itself.

Nothing happened during the day, so I gave him the details of what happened with the incident. I finished by telling him that I locked Moki in his kennel for the night, although he usually sleeps on the couch. I told him that Moki always came into my room to my bed to say good night to me, and came into my room to my bed to say good morning to me. After what happened with him, I felt too afraid for him to come to my bed.

Aha moment! My eyes lit up with discovery when I looked at Ryan! There was no molestation! I was afraid of *Moki* coming to my bed! Phew! How I hate clichés!

Ryan asked if I was afraid at those times when Moki was afraid of the other dog. Yes, I was. I knew how the dog affected him, and that did scare me. Ryan also said there was probably other fear as well. He said that when a woman is outside alone at night, it is natural to feel somewhat afraid. If you add in that I live in the wilderness and the threat of mountain lions and bears is a real possibility, yes, I was afraid. Every night when I went outside, those possibilities were on my mind. He said that was perfectly understandable.

Next, Ryan wanted me to give him a statement of how I felt as Moki was biting me. I felt scared. I felt terrified. Then, Ryan wanted a positive statement to attach to it. So, I said, "I am brave. I am courageous. I am fearless."

Ryan asked, "How realistic is that? Could you really feel fearless in a situation like that?"

"No!" I laughed. He suggested, "I can feel safe." That was probably as close as it was going to get!

When it came time to do the EMDR, I wanted to go back to the eye movement instead of the earphones and hand vibrators that we used the first time. Although studies have shown that all methods have successful outcomes, the eye movement had a slightly higher success rate. My ex-husband used the earphones, though, and the changes in him were remarkable. Still, I chose the eye movement.

Ryan asked what part of the extreme biting incident scared me the most. My reply was when Moki first leaped at me and started biting. He wanted to know on a scale of one to ten how it felt and where in my body I felt it. It was a ten bursting at the seams, and I felt it in my heart and solar plexus.

The idea was to feel the feeling as Ryan moved his fingers in front of me. The first thing that happened was the feeling moved up into my throat. It made me wonder if I had even verbalized to Moki to stop, and I didn't think I did. Ryan felt that although I backed up during the incident, I just froze. And I felt that was an apt description.

We did the eye movements for twenty or thirty seconds. Then we assessed where I was on the scale of one to ten with the body feelings. We would also see "what came up." I was familiar with something "coming up" from my off and on use of EFT. And something had unexpectedly "come up" a couple of weeks earlier when I first started working with EFT on the fear issues.

As I tapped for feeling afraid, an image of me at ten years old popped up. I was with a neighbor boy, Buddy, and we had walked up to the corner. The corner property had a tall hedge around it, with tiny flowers here and there. A bunch of small moths flitted from flower to flower. Buddy showed me how to catch a moth, throw it down against the pavement, and then cut its head off. I did it a few times and didn't like it at all. It didn't sit right with me, and it still bothers me now as I write about it. When I told a friend about this, she said it sounded like a boy thing.

What that image popping up meant to me, was that along with the fear issues with Moki, I had to deal with thinking that using the choke chain on him was cruel. Killing those moths like that was cruel, and somehow my brain connected the two events.

Back to the EMDR, we did the eye movements and worked on whatever came up and assessed each step. I finally got down to a seven on Moki's lunging. Then, during one eye movement session, it went down to six, then five, then back up to six. As all this happened, I analyzed every step. I told Ryan about that and said that I knew it made his job harder. He said that analyzing everything like that was a control issue. Earlier in my life —well, not too much earlier—I had many control issues. But I thought I had mostly gotten rid of them. Apparently not.

What I thought about during that six to five to six session was why wasn't I willing to let this go? And what kind of strokes did I get from keeping it inside me? Ryan smiled and said he had wondered about blocking issues and just in case had printed and brought along a Blocking Beliefs Questionnaire.

That was my homework. My other homework was to have a plan in case Moki started the extreme biting again. I thought I would ask Jade for help with that.

At the end of the session, I felt better. As I walked out, Ryan said that I seemed more relaxed than when I walked in. After leaving his office, I drove to the post office. As I stepped out of the car and walked in, I felt like my steps were lighter. I felt different. Had something really shifted in me, or did I feel that way because Ryan said that I seemed more relaxed?

When I got home, Moki wanted to go outside. I leashed him up, and we walked out. As he peed, I heard something above us. On the balcony, the exuberant teenaged puppy looked down. I felt no fear. Moki looked up and sniffed the air. As soon as I realized that I felt no fear, a small spike of fear shot through me, but noticeably lighter than anything before. Granted, he wasn't as threatening above us as on the ground where Moki could see him clearly, and yet it still felt like a small step forward.

Throughout the rest of the day, little things that ordinarily might set my fear off, gave me a little charge, but not much. And I enlarged on my kiva safe place. I imagined myself going down the ladder into the kiva. As I took each step closer to the bottom, I relaxed more and more. I *loved* that kiva image!

Later that night, Moki heard a noise from upstairs. He gave a small bark and looked at me expectantly. At a time like that, it was my job as pack leader to remain calm and reassure him. I told him everything was okay and there was nothing to worry about. I said it a couple times as I looked at him. Then, spontaneously, he jumped up, wagged his tail, and went to get his ball. He believed me when I told him everything was all right! We were making progress!

Following Instructions

I felt no fear throughout the day. Of course, there was nothing to be fearful of, but that usually didn't stop me! Then, the last walk of the night, Moki kept watching down the driveway. When I followed where he was looking, I saw Addie, a neighbor dog, come bounding toward us. I put myself between them and kept telling her to go home. She didn't know what to do. As Jade had instructed, I kept Moki behind me, so that I stayed between the two dogs. When I stole a quick glance in Moki's direction, he had his tail up and looked happy, not fearful. I kept telling Addie to go home. She wagged her tail and didn't have a clue. Finally, she ran upstairs to where the other dogs lived. But I knew the gate was closed, and she'd be coming back down.

When I was in Boulder, Jade gave me a human analogy. If you are in the mall eating lunch with a friend, and your old boyfriend, who you're not quite over, walks by with his new girlfriend, it's a dicey situation. You're glaring at them and getting more and more upset. If you continue to sit there watching them, you're going to feel worse and worse. But, if you get up and walk away, you will feel better almost immediately.

So, taking that as our cue, I decided not to just stand there and let Addie come running back out to us. Moki wasn't going to poop with Addie running around, so we might as well go in. Hurriedly, I started walking Moki toward the passageway to our door. Just then, Addie bounded down the stairs. Hoping that Addie wouldn't follow, I pulled Moki after me. She didn't.

I did feel afraid during the incident. Was I as afraid as I used to be? I didn't think so; I thought it felt significantly less. Moki didn't seem put off by my unstable energy pattern, so I hoped that it didn't "show" too much.

Back to the Kiva

I had been doing so well, and then everything fell apart. There had been no need to go to my kiva safe place for a couple days, and I felt excited about that. I didn't know what changed, but I felt I needed the kiva again. That was disappointing. It only got worse from there.

Moki had been resisting putting on the Gentle Leader, but I had mostly cornered him and put it on him, anyway. I thought it might be something that I should be afraid of, but I wasn't. Then, I decided that he shouldn't fight me like that. Next time he asked to go out and refused to let me put it on, I took off my coat and sat back down. Moki was incredibly smart, so I figured he would understand that if he wanted to go out, then he needed to be cooperative with the Gentle Leader. After two false starts, he still wasn't cooperative.

Since he had drunk a great deal of water, I knew he needed to go outside. So I put on my coat and held out the Gentle Leader for him to put his nose in (like he did for Jade in the motel room). He wouldn't. Then, I felt a rush of fear and couldn't get near him. I kneeled and went to the kiva safe place and tried to calm myself down. I was afraid of what my unstable energy would do to Moki. He gave me a look, but not the unstable energy alert look. That was good. After I did some deep breathing and I thought of the kiva for a few minutes, Moki pressed into me and I slipped the Gentle Leader on him. At that moment, I knew that I couldn't use the Gentle Leader again until I stabilized my energy. I didn't think it would be soon.

The previous day and a half of living with no discernible fear was like breathing fresh air for the first time. Having the fear come back was a terrible disappointment.

The last time we went out for the night, I thought maybe I could get the Gentle Leader on after all. We walked over to where I keep the leashes. I looked at him, and he gave me a look like, "Don't even think about it!" I sighed and grabbed the regular leash. When he saw it, he wagged his tail. He had won. Unfortunately.

Before going to sleep, I sent an email off to Jade telling her of my two steps backwards. I also confessed that I had been too afraid (even on the fear-free days) to hook Moki's leash to my belt like she had suggested when we were in Boulder.

More Leash Troubles

It was spitting snow when Moki and I took our morning walk. I put on his regular leash and connected it to his collar. He was happy and wagging, so it didn't scare me.

While walking, I didn't feel the previous night's fear even when I corrected him. In my most fearful times, even giving him a small correction scared me because I didn't know how he would react. So it was good that I felt no fear. I had to keep reminding myself that this journey to healing that Moki and I were taking was not on a linear path.

The rest of the day, I felt off, but not afraid. Although I had no reason to feel afraid, that never stopped me before! I wondered if the "fear-attack" from the previous day had been a fluke.

Then came time for our afternoon walk. It went well. Moki did everything he was supposed to do, and I did everything I was supposed to do. The most fragile times for me were putting the leash on and taking the leash off. Putting the leash on him that afternoon had been easy. He wagged his tail and wanted to go out. Taking it off was another matter.

We walked into the house, me first with him following. He took a couple steps away from me. Leaning down to take off the leash, I immediately felt a rush of fear. I managed to get the leash off, but he stood there without moving, looking at me accusingly. He felt my unstable energy and wasn't comfortable with it. His uncomfortable look scared me even more, because I didn't know how to handle it. It didn't feel right sending Moki to his kennel, because he hadn't done anything wrong—I had. I should've sent myself to the kennel! Instead, I told him to go get his ball. It broke the spell, he wagged his tail and bounded off, and I was okay again. If I could call it okay. The incident bothered me.

When he wanted to go out in the early evening, I put on his leash before I put on my coat. I didn't want the scary anticipation of putting on his leash to affect my energy. We walked outside and I heard a dog or dogs loose down the way. So we had to find a new potty area close to our building, so the other dogs wouldn't see us and approach. He finished, and we walked back inside. I wanted to unhook his leash right before the interior door. I thought that way I could handle it. I'd get it unhooked before the fear feelings overcame me. But Moki tricked me. He stopped wagging his tail and looked at me expectantly. It was like he expected my energy to get unstable, and he was right. We walked into the house with him still leashed, and he just looked at me. Scared, I did the only logical thing I could think of: I told him to get his ball. Excitedly, he wagged his tail and fetched his ball. Leaning down to touch the ball, I rapidly unhooked his leash.

Another scary situation averted. And I knew it was all me. That made me feel bad. And I felt even worse because two days earlier I had had a taste of what it was like to be fear-free. I wanted that feeling again.

But I felt like I was going so far backwards, that I wasn't sure if I could get forward momentum again. I felt defeated.

Since Jade usually wrote back to me right away, I felt uneasy that she hadn't answered my email about not being able to put the Gentle Leader on. Just in case she didn't get the email, I sent it back with a note that my troubles with the leash had increased.

Gentle Leader Difficulties

In the morning, I checked my email to see if I had received anything from Jade. I did. The reason she hadn't written back right away like she usually did was because she was trying to reach Janice. She wanted to find out what to do to make me more comfortable with the leash and Gentle Leader. Since they were essential items, they couldn't be something that were associated with fear for either Moki or me.

Jade suggested leaving the situation altogether instead of getting the ball and increasing the energy level. She said that he doesn't have to get the leash on or off right away. I should pick up the leash with the Gentle Leader and put it on him like it is nothing. And if I felt myself getting afraid, I should drop it and walk away. After I calmed myself down, I should try again, even if it took a few tries. She said this was really important because Moki must trust me to be stable enough to work with him. Jade ended the email by saying, "You can do this. Moki needs you to do this."

Although I understood Jade's words, in the morning I didn't have enough time to suppress my fear and coax Moki into the Gentle Leader. Because of the possibility of other dogs, I needed to get to the hiking place early. So I had to get him leashed right away and start our walk.

Our morning walk was fine using the regular leash. When we approached our door, I didn't think that I could take it off, so I let him inside with the leash still on. After removing my coat, hat, and gloves, I sat at my desk. He came over all wagging, and I unhooked the leash with no problem. It was a workaround, but it was the best I could do right then.

Since I still felt upset about having those two fear-free days and then taking a giant leap backwards, I wrote to Ryan asking him if it was "normal." Ryan wrote back that he was happy about the fear-free days and it was definitely progress. He said that it's tough when a trigger brings it back, but it is all normal. He said it means that we are moving in the right direction, but still have more work to do. Ryan suggested using my safe place and my EFT to calm down; and he said that learning to cope with fear is part of the journey.

Everything he said gave me great relief. Although I had great confidence in EMDR to heal me, I knew it would take more than two sessions. I felt like what I was going through was just part of the process, but sometimes a person needs reassuring.

Later that day, I took the Gentle Leader and put it over by my desk. I asked Moki if he wanted to go out, and I held out the Gentle Leader loop. He looked at me and walked away. I beckoned to him several times, but I acted a little giddy—my way of not feeling afraid—so it didn't work. Then he rang the bell at the door to go outside. When I held out the Gentle Leader again, he still wouldn't come around. Or, he would come around and give me his body like in a hug instead of his face. I realized that my energy was too high, so I calmed myself down. Moki came over and put his face in the loop! When I had initially brought the leash and Gentle Leader over to my desk, I was afraid that if I couldn't get it on him, I was enabling him to "win." And I knew that wouldn't be good. Thankfully, it all worked out well.

After we came back inside, I wrote Jade a quick note about what happened and my success. She wrote back and said that was a big step. Ah, a small fragment of satisfaction.

Sometime that afternoon, Moki drank a great deal of water and ate some salad. Instead of going to the door and ringing the bell as he usually did, he walked over to my desk where the Gentle Leader was and barked. I sat at my desk and held out the Gentle Leader, but immediately felt scared, so he wouldn't give me his face. Focusing on my kiva safe place, I tried to calm down. Meanwhile, he chased after his ball and bounded up to me wagging. After playing with him for a minute, I grabbed the Gentle Leader and put it on him.

The reason I had been using getting the ball to diffuse the situation was because when he got the ball, his tail would wag and my fears would evaporate. So this time, *he* diffused the situation to get my energy more stable. I may be giving Moki too much credit, but I felt convinced that he did that deliberately—*knowing* that getting the ball stabilized *my* energy. What a dog!

A Growl and a Questionnaire

For our first walk of the morning, I put on the regular leash for speed's sake. The rest of our walks all day were with the Gentle Leader. I'd hold it out, and he'd look at me. If he walked away or laid down, I'd put it down. Then he'd ask to go out again, and I'd hold it up again. The first time he eventually wagged and put his nose in the loop. The second time, he was more reluctant but eventually did it. As the day wore on though, I became less and less sure of myself.

Moki wanted to go out shortly after eating dinner. I used the regular leash because my fear had increased during the day. As we walked out to where he pees, I heard the dogs upstairs. They had been there a few times in the last couple weeks, and it hadn't been a problem. I would usually say hello to them, and Moki would ignore them. But after I said hello, and when Moki finished peeing, he growled at them. My first thought was to say, "no" and move him away from them. So I took him across the driveway to where he normally goes to poop. It felt like an extremely inflammable situation.

After he finished, I knew we still had to go under the dogs to get back to our door. There was no choice.

And I knew I needed to keep my energy stable while I did it. That was critical. The situation was too close to the one that created Moki's extreme biting.

I brought Moki to my side and walked briskly across the driveway without looking up at the dogs on the deck. We were through the tough part! Moki showed no reaction, and we made it to our door safely. As we walked into the house, I dropped the leash and didn't take it off until later.

Once inside the house, we both settled down almost immediately. I felt grateful that it turned out as well as it had. I also felt a certain sense of accomplishment that I may have prevented something that could have been bad. After I calmed down, I emailed Jade to ask her what I should have done in that situation.

What Ryan had written to me the previous day came to mind: "Learning to cope when the fear comes is part of the journey." I guess I thought that EMDR was like a magic pill: take it and all the fear disappears. When it's really a team effort: while the EMDR is working, I must work, too—pushing down the unreasonable fears and not letting them affect me. It must be like meditating. If a thought comes when you meditate, you gently brush it aside and go back to your meditation. So when a fear thought came, I needed to gently brush it aside and go back to what I was doing. Although I don't want to argue for my limitations here, letting the fear thoughts go sounds easier than it is.

Since it was only a couple more days until my next EMDR appointment, I thought I'd better get my homework done. First, I filled out the Blocking Beliefs Questionnaire. It consisted of twenty-five one-sentence statements that I had to answer with a number from one (feels completely untrue) to a seven (feels completely true). Most of my answers were ones and twos, with a three, a five, and a six. The five was, "I'm embarrassed that I have this problem." And the six was, "I don't want to think about this problem anymore."

For the first statement, I think I felt more embarrassed that I was stupid enough to create the problem. For the second statement, I *didn't* want to think about this problem anymore. I wanted it to be finished and in the past.

The other part of the homework was what I asked Jade to help me with. I needed to come up with a plan that would make me feel safe in case the extreme biting ever happened again.

All I could think of was the video of the famous dog whisperer kicking at that dog that was biting him to get it to stop. That's not what I wanted to do. I felt that I had inflicted enough pain on Moki already with my one big mistake that caused all this in the first place. That's something that I didn't want to do again. And I also didn't want to focus on him doing that again. The thought of that manifested unstable and fearful energy. So I took a proactive approach—suggested by Jade—which completely resonated with me. Instead of what I would do if it happened, I would tell what I was doing to keep it from ever happening again.

This is what I wrote: Under my dog whisperer's guidance, I have put many things into place to insure the extreme biting doesn't happen again. In following her advice, Moki and I are building the trust and respect needed for a healthy pack. My plan is to create a purpose for Moki and me, to set rules and boundaries based on respect in order to build trust, and to create a stronger connection between us.

Don't Look Now

The previous evening's event showed me two things: one, how far I'd come; and two, how far I still needed to go. Because I saw a person with a dog ahead of us on the trail, we cut our morning walk short. I decided not to use the Gentle Leader again until after my next EMDR session. It triggered my fear. And Moki and I were getting along fine without the Gentle Leader—and the fear.

After Moki ate his breakfast and asked to go out, I put his regular leash on him, and we walked outside. He didn't need to pee in his regular spot—underneath the deck and the two dogs—so we walked past it and continued across the driveway. While he was out there sniffing around, I saw that the two dogs had returned to the deck. So it would be another thrill ride to get to my door. I knew I could do it. When Moki finished, I pulled him to my side and walked briskly toward our door. I ignored the upstairs dogs, and when I sneaked a quick glance toward Moki, he showed no reaction to them at all. Another success.

When I was in Boulder with Jade, she talked to me about not looking at Moki when I corrected him. I listened and didn't ask her to elaborate on it. But the book she had given me talked about it a great deal and gave me much more information. It made me realize that part of the trigger the night of the extreme biting might have been me looking at Moki.

The previous night when I had to get away from the upstairs dogs, I did not look at him when I pulled him away. Except for a quick and hopefully surreptitious glance in his direction while we walked, I didn't look at him as we walked briskly back to the door, either.

Donald Who?

My EMDR appointment took an unexpected twist. We started with me feeling the feeling of the extreme biting—the initial lunge, specifically—in my heart area. I watched Ryan's fingers go rapidly from side to side and then felt the feeling move up to my throat. I could barely swallow. What came up during that session was a memory of something that happened to me when I was thirty. While I was living in Maine, I traveled back to California to visit my mother. A friend and I went to Disneyland, and I bought a Donald Duck hat. At the end of my trip when I prepared to leave for the airport, I wore the hat. My mother said some rather unkind words to me about wearing the hat—words that have haunted me ever since. It surprised me that it came up, because I thought I had resolved that issue several years before.

Ryan wanted to know why I was defending my mother for saying those unkind words to me. I told him that I knew my mother did her best and that she didn't hurt me deliberately. So I had forgiven her. Ryan said that even if somebody doesn't do something deliberately, it can still really hurt and cause damage. My response was that I knew if someone accidentally drove over a person, even if they didn't mean to, the person was still dead. And yes, I knew there was damage done —especially since those words still haunted me after all these years. But I felt that my mother should be forgiven.

Then, my eyes brightened and I smiled. A revelation! I told Ryan that if I can forgive my mother for some bad things that she had done to me, then I should be able to forgive myself for what I'd done to Moki. That was huge for me.

We also talked about my difficulty talking to strangers. That was something that I had written off to my insecurity and introversion. I would never have spent the time or effort to go to a therapist about that. Now, I was there to help my relationship with my dog, and "talking" unexpectedly came up. And now it would be healed, too. How cool is that!

Later in our session, as I visualized the lunging part of the extreme biting, I felt as if I were an observer. Then, it felt like I watched it from faraway. The whole scene was changing right in front of my eyes. This healing business was interesting stuff. Ryan said it was going well.

That evening, when we first walked outside, the neighbor from the top floor, Tim, was walking from his car. Moki jumped right up on him and licked his face. Tim petted him, and I apologized. Jade told me that jumping was a dominant behavior and only a pack leader would do that. She said that once I firmly prove myself as pack leader, then Moki should understand that all people are above all dogs. Then, he should stop doing that. I would be glad when Moki's respect for humans kicked in so he wouldn't jump on people anymore. Moki is a big boy. Not only did his jumping embarrass me, but he could hurt someone who didn't expect it.

All is Well

    While I made the salad, I set aside some vegetables to give Moki after I finished eating. Before I finished making the salad, the timer bell rang for the main meal. After eating that, I returned to finish the salad. It only needed a couple other vegetables cut up and added into it. Since I planned to eat the salad later, I gave Moki his vegetables. Less than five minutes after that, I decided that I wanted the salad after all. So I ate it. I wasn't sure if it was my imagination or not, but Moki gave me a funny look. Immediately, I realized that for him, he saw the situation as me feeding him first. Not a good mistake to make when the situation between us was still so tenuous.
    An hour before his dinnertime, we took our late afternoon walk. He hadn't gone out for a while, so he really had to pee. We walked over to where we usually walk, and he peed and peed. At the same time, he looked around and found something to get excited about. I didn't know what it was. He barked and barked. First I tried to lead him away and distract him, but he kept looking back at whatever it was he thought he saw. I thought it might be a big rock or a road sign.

Since I couldn't get his attention and he kept barking, I took him away from our usual spot and walked him up and down the driveway. Luckily, no other dogs were out at the time.

When I wrote to Jade about the rock, she said I made the right move by getting him away from the situation. She said that he shouldn't get worked up over it again, unless *I* think about it. I should always keep him moving if he gets focused on something. The body follows the mind, so I needed to keep both moving.

I finally sent the email that I had written to Bill a week earlier. In the email, I told Bill how fragile my relationship with Moki was. And how much everything had changed in one week. While I didn't feel confident enough to say that our relationship was stable, it wasn't unstable anymore, either. We were on the way to stability, and we had a running start. How grateful I felt for this perspective.

Sometimes when we were inside, Moki would hear a noise and look up or even give a small bark. When we were at the motel, Jade said that I should go to the window, check it out, and then assure Moki that all was well. That was what I did at home whenever he heard the noise. I would stand up, go to the window and the door, listen and look, and then tell him that it was okay. He would get so happy afterward, wagging and smiling. It's like that was exactly what he needed from me.

I felt our relationship growing stronger and more solid. As my fears slowly evaporated, I felt better about him, which in turn made him feel better about me. He wagged his tail much more often.

Something that Janice mentioned to me on the phone during our last conversation was not to walk over or around Moki if he was in my way. I told her that I couldn't step over him because I was too afraid. But I didn't realize how often I walked around him. She said it was very important that he give up the space to the pack leader. When I first started asking him to move, he did, but he looked like he resented it. Later, he acted much more accepting of the new rule and didn't seem to mind too much. So many changes were happening in our lives.

Loose Dog!

While I was in town grocery shopping, I ran into a friend whom I hadn't seen for a long time. She told me about her dog, and how it was the best dog she'd ever had. After the conversation covered other topics, I described the issues that I'd had with Moki.

Then, she told me more about her dog. When they first got him, he would get up on the bed and growl and snap at them when they tried to get him off. Her husband would grab him by the collar and pull him off the bed. He asserted that *he* was pack leader. She didn't say how long this went on, but showing the dog who the pack leader was had "fixed" the dog. Their family included a twelve-year-old and a toddler. They could have given this dog back when he first growled. Instead, they affirmed their roles as pack leader, and the dog turned out to be wonderful. What a great story!

Late in the afternoon, Moki and I took our walk. I decided to try our regular spot and hope that he had forgotten about the "threatening" rock or sign. I walked quickly up there and kept walking. He followed and had forgotten all about the threat from the day before just like Jade said he would.

After eating dinner, Moki asked to go outside. I hooked up the leash, opened the door, and there at the end of the passageway leading to my apartment stood Cooper. Instantly, I pulled Moki back into the house and closed our door. Then, I stepped back outside and told Cooper to go home. He immediately ran upstairs. Since I didn't know if Pete had been outside with him, I chose to wait.

An hour later, I walked outside to see if there were any dogs out. When I didn't see any, I hooked Moki back up, and we walked outside. While I was out there, the upstairs neighbor, Steve, who owns the dogs, walked by. I said hello and asked how he was. He answered and asked how I was. But it was barely civil, not like he usually was. My guess was that he was upset about having to keep his dogs in. Since it was almost the end of the month and I had to talk to them about giving me another dog-free month, I decided I had better do it sooner than later. But I would try to approach Hildy on her day off the following week.

Manipulation!

Moki had started something new. It felt like manipulation and it felt like he was winning. I didn't think it was good. Because it was less scary to me for some reason, I was taking his leash off in our mudroom just outside our front door. Moki would stand there and not follow me in. So I would have to call him in. Sometimes I thought it would be better to leave him out there, so I did. Then, I wouldn't let him in until he scratched on the door a couple times. But it didn't feel right. I wrote to Jade about it.

Jade suggested walking him all the way inside instead of stopping in the mudroom. That way, I am making the decision and not him. It's his job to follow me, so he needs to walk calmly behind me into the room. Also, I am claiming the room, the situation, and Moki.

I Don't Want to Be Afraid Anymore

In the morning when I reached for Moki's leash, instead of taking his regular leash which I did every morning, my first thought was, "I don't want to be afraid anymore." So I reached for the Gentle Leader, put it on him, and we walked out the door.

Later that evening, I tried something. For the previous year, if Moki was lying on the couch and I touched something near him, he would jump up and maybe growl, or look suspiciously and then jump off the couch. Earlier than that if it happened, he would definitely growl and sometimes snap. Since I didn't want to upset him, I always said his name before picking up a book near him. But now that we were healing, I tried it and he looked up, not threatening or suspicious, just curious. And all was okay. Another huge change in Moki.

An hour before we went to sleep as I worked at my desk, my feet rested on the legs of the chair. Moki, as usual, was right on the floor beneath me. When I unconsciously put my foot down and gently stepped on him, he made a noise that wasn't quite a growl. I looked at him and said, "Sorry," but he was completely okay with it. He started wagging his tail and ran to get his ball. It was like he was saying, "I know you didn't do that on purpose, so let's play!" There was not a hint of fear or suspicion in him. More progress.

Usually if I was on the phone and one of those corporate answering machines answered, "Tap or say 'one'," I always used to tap. Earlier in the day when I was on the phone, I said, "one"! Success! You may think this is small, but for me—someone who claimed to be "not verbal"—it was huge. Another growth-filled day for both of us! The EMDR *was* helping my talking issues!

They Called the Sheriff (But They Only Got the Deputy)

Since it was close to the end of the month—and I had found Cooper loose the other day—I thought I should go talk to the people upstairs to ask for another dog-free month. I wanted to talk to Hildy while Steve was at work—for various reasons including his coolness a few days earlier. When I heard their children running around in the morning, I walked outside to knock on their door and talk to Hildy. As I walked out of my passageway, I saw Steve and the two dogs loose in the yard. I said hello and asked if Hildy was home. Then, I asked if I could talk to both of them together. He didn't look at me and said he had some stuff to do, but he'd be up soon. I stood there and waited. When I saw him put the dogs upstairs and go in, I walked to their front door and knocked.

When Hildy answered, I asked if I could talk to Steve, too. She said he was busy with the kids. Since he had just stepped into the house, he was obviously avoiding me. When I started by saying that I knew he was upset about the situation, she agreed. Although they have a fenced yard their dogs can play in, they were not happy with keeping their dogs in. I described a hypothetical scary scenario to her involving their children to see if she could feel the fear I felt whenever I ventured out and saw their dogs. Before that, I said something that she misinterpreted. I made reference to my "vicious" dog and her children. It wasn't a threat, but it could have been perceived as one. It was something that I would later regret.

Hildy said they chose to live here so their dogs could run loose; and everybody else in the area allowed their dogs to run loose. When I mentioned their dogs had been out a couple times that week, she said those were the only times. Right. I didn't believe her. Those were just the times that I caught them out. I doubted very much if those were the only times. Hildy said they were doing their best. Right, again. The dogs were not escaping. Someone was opening the door and deliberately letting them out. Trying is lying. Just don't let them out.

The whole conversation felt horrible. I walked downstairs to my apartment, and I yelled, screamed, and acted unstable, which is exactly how I felt. Moki, who would normally give me the unstable energy alert at a time like that, immediately came up to me and comforted me. My unstable energy didn't frighten him.

When I told Jade about it later, she said that he was starting to trust me again. He's very sensitive to my moods. It was progress for us that he chose to comfort me instead of becoming fearful.

Mostly, I was upset because the people upstairs didn't get it. They didn't understand what was at stake, and they obviously couldn't "feel my pain." There was nothing I could do about the situation. I felt powerless to change their ignorant behavior. It felt bad.

After settling down from the conversation, I asked myself if I was wrong in asking them to keep their dogs in. Was it an inappropriate request? Was I asking too much? I'm sure they thought I violated their rights by asking. And yes, it had already been a month and a half.

But I didn't feel the request was too much. After all, I told them that I wanted to move out and had been searching for another apartment, which was true. And they had a fenced yard where their dogs could run around. Maybe it *was* wrong of me to ask them to keep their dogs in. I still don't know.

Later, when I was outside walking Moki, Hildy drove up, got out of the truck, walked over to me, and asked to talk—not in a nice way. She said she just filed a complaint with our landlord because I threatened them. I denied doing that, and she started screaming at me. I told her that I needed to put Moki inside but I would come right back out. Although Hildy's outburst had already upset him, I got him inside safely.

When I went back outside, she yelled and yelled. She said I didn't even thank them for keeping the dogs in all this time. I'm a "thank you" person. If anything, I say it too much. I told her that I had said that I appreciated it. She said that I didn't say that until she pointed it out. What she didn't realize, and what I was too upset to mention at the time, was that if the dogs were out "sometimes," that meant I had to be afraid *every time* I went outside—because I wouldn't know when they were out and when they were not. The unknown is sometimes worse than the known.

Then Steve came out of the house, and he yelled, too. There wasn't much I could do. I am not perfect. I am flawed, and those last weeks had been a big strain on me trying to hold everything together. So I uttered an obscene comment to Steve. He replied in kind and then said he was going to call the sheriff and report me for threatening them.

The first thing that I felt I needed to do was to tell my side of the story to the landlord. So I drove up to his place of business to talk to him. He said that he didn't want to get involved, and he said that's exactly what he had told Hildy. Phew. At least that was fine. Then when

I got home, I immediately called the sheriff. The dispatcher took my name and number.

The deputy called back in half an hour. As I told him the whole story, he interrupted now and then to ask a question or make a comment. At that point, I was barely able to hold it together, and he could tell. His calmness helped me. He was very objective about the situation, and I told him that I appreciated that. He said even though I hadn't made an overt threat, what I did say was designed to scare someone. That was against the law. Oh, great, now I'm a lawbreaker. The deputy said that where we live, if dogs are in visual range and a voice command will control them, then it's legal for them to be loose. The night of the extreme biting, both dogs were loose and no one was around. But I was too distraught to tell him that. He said he'd call the people and call me back. I asked him to please apologize for me.

When he called me back, he said they are not going to press charges, so he didn't have to write me a ticket. That was a blessing. I again told him that I appreciated his objectivity; he said he hoped I had a better rest of the day, and we hung up. I cried.

When I had spoken with a friend earlier in the week about the dogs being out, she said that when I go out there and the dogs are loose, that would be my graduation. It looked like graduation day was coming sooner rather than later.

Blame It on the EMDR!

In the middle of the night, I awoke with what felt like perfect clarity. The essence of the matter was that I was afraid when the neighbor's dogs ran loose outside. It did not matter why I was afraid. It did not matter that I was afraid of what the dogs might trigger in Moki, and in turn what would happen to me because of it. The important fact was that I was afraid when their dogs ran loose outside. That should have been enough to persuade them to keep their dogs in—consideration of my fear—no matter the reason. My neighbors lacked the compassion needed for them to honor that request. I had a right to be upset with their lack of consideration.

I wanted to tell that and several other things to the deputy. On the night of the extreme biting, their dogs ran loose for almost ten minutes—the whole time I was out there—while Steve was in the house. The dogs were not in visual or voice command range. I wasn't sure if Steve told the deputy that he was outside with them, but I believed that was what the deputy understood.

Also, I wanted to tell him how everything started with Pete when he and his brother, now gone, rushed

Moki one foot outside our doorway with no one around to call them off. That was another time they were loose without being in visual and voice command range. And that's when Moki's fear of Pete began. And Pete kept getting bigger.

I also recalled an incredibly ludicrous comment by Hildy. We were talking about how the dogs being in that narrow passageway and blocking Moki's exit scared him. She said, "What do you expect us to do? Not go into our storage unit?" I said, "No, just don't bring the dogs with you when you go in there." Duh.

My EMDR appointment turned out very interesting, as usual. After I told Ryan the whole story of the day before and my poor choice of saying bad things to the neighbors, his response surprised me. He said there was a good chance the EMDR caused my poor choice. He said that since I was learning to "be verbal" again, I needed to learn what was appropriate and what was inappropriate. It's a skill that I still needed to learn as I became more verbal.

From there, we started working again on the extreme biting incident. It wasn't long before the emotional "charge" attached to the incident was almost gone. When Ryan asked me to visualize the moment Moki first lunged at me, which had been the most upsetting image, it felt like the image itself had faded. It was almost completely gone. Then, when we did the positive statement, "I am learning to be kind, courageous, and verbal," the number that I assigned how true it felt—one to seven—felt strongly like a six or a seven. I am learning how to be kind, courageous, and verbal!

During this session and my previous session when we worked on positive statements, Ryan used a slow back and forth finger movement. I asked him why. He said the fast movements had proven more effective for desensitization purposes. But the slow movements were more effective for ingraining the positive statements and beliefs.

First Contact

I drove into town intending to visit the deputy that I spoke with a couple days before. When I inquired in the sheriff's office, they didn't even know whom I had spoken with. Since no one filed a complaint, nothing was on record. They said they'd try to figure out who I had spoken to and have him call me. He never called. Instead of pursuing it, I decided that I didn't have to prove that I was right. I already knew I was.

The two items that I wanted to clarify with the deputy were part of what he and I had discussed that day, but that I had been in no condition at the time to dispute. One was that the deputy said I demanded the neighbors keep their dogs inside. Demanded? I would say I "asked" but it was closer to begging than asking. I knew it was asking much of them, and I felt I needed to plead with them so they would comply.

The second item was that the loose dogs had to be in voice and visual range. It seemed like Steve had told the deputy his dogs were in that range the night the extreme biting happened. The dogs were out loose by themselves for almost ten minutes before Steve called them in. Had Steve been watching and the dogs were "in visual range" he would have called them in sooner. These two items were possibly lies that Steve told the deputy. That made me want to clarify the story. But it wasn't meant to be. I knew in my heart the truth, and that was all that mattered.

That afternoon as I walked Moki, one of his doggie friends, Addie, came running up to us. In the past weeks, every time I saw her approaching, I would take Moki into the house. This time, I decided it was time to just wait. When she approached Moki, he did not have his ruff up, but his tail was up. I knew he was not afraid, and I knew that Addie was harmless. They sniffed noses, and all was okay. My first test with another dog. We were progressing.

Meanwhile, Moki wagged his tail more and more—especially at times when he never wagged before. It felt good. And more and more often when he rolled onto his back, he opened both legs for me to scratch his tummy. More and more progress, and it felt good.

A Trip and a Relapse

After the preliminary counseling session, three EMDR sessions, and the episode with the deputy, I decided to leave the state. For more than two months, I had been looking for a new place to rent in town. After finding nothing, nothing, and more nothing, it looked like it was time to leave. There were many places to rent in my new chosen town. Driving down there and renting something was the next order of business.

When Moki and I took a brief drive down there, our schedules and daily activities were slightly off. I walked him and ate, but not my whole meal. Then I would feed him, and sometimes I would eat again after that. He often jumped up on the motel bed. Although I always made him get off when I got on, I usually invited him back up. When I slept, he would often sleep on the bed as well. At first, if I moved, he would immediately get off the bed. A few months ago, he might have growled before getting off, but at this point, he just got uncomfortable and jumped off. The last night at the motel, he stayed on the bed most of the night. And sometimes when I walked him, I would let him walk in front. Although I usually noticed within thirty seconds and then made him walk beside me.

So I didn't know if it was the weird schedule, the little discrepancies in our behavior program, or just the unstable energy of the moving trip that caused a new incident. I had always been scared when Moki was in the backseat of my car. I think he felt cornered there. And I learned years before not to try to pet him when he was back there. But at this point in our recovery, I thought it was safe to do so and that it would benefit the new fear-free me to try it. The first time was hard, but I did it. I looked at him, reached back, and stroked his head. Several more times in the few days away, I did that. But on our way home, after having already petted him in the backseat many times, I reached over my left shoulder without looking at him, he came up, and I scratched his head. Suddenly, he growled and snapped at me.

Since I had reached behind me, he could have easily bitten me, but he didn't. Still, it bothered me. We had come so far without any relapse, and now this. And Moki stood in the backseat with a watchful awareness to see if I would do anything else to scare him. And that scared me. I tilted back the rearview mirror so I could watch him.

After a while, I decided it would be good to take him outside the car and walk him. I thought that might break the tension for both of us. That did some good, but afterward Moki still seemed to have a watchful awareness which kept me on edge.

After the next stop when we walked, everything seemed healed. Still, I didn't feel good about it. To have come more than a month without incident and then have this happen, bothered me. And I hadn't had enough sleep the previous night, which always made these situations worse. I needed to write to Jade and get her take on it.

Later that evening back in Colorado, Moki flopped down next to me exposing his whole belly for me to scratch—a very trusting thing to do.   It was like what Jade told me—dogs live in the moment. He had already completely forgotten about the car incident.

Amazing EMDR

Directly after the snapping incident in the car, I had thought I wouldn't be putting on the Gentle Leader for a while. But the following morning, I decided that if Moki could forget about it so quickly, then so could I. I put on the Gentle Leader with no trouble. That was a *huge* difference for me. After a growling or biting incident, it used to take me days before I got over it. This new change in me felt amazing. I liked it.

My EMDR appointment was amazing, too. First, Ryan had me close my eyes and visualize the entire extreme biting incident again. He said whenever I got to a place that made me uncomfortable, I should stop and open my eyes. My first stop was Moki's initial lunge toward me. That image bothered me more than anything else right from the beginning, and that was where our focus had been. It still bothered me. But on a scale from one to ten, I gave it a five instead of eight or ten where it started.

Then Ryan wanted to know a negative statement about myself concerning the incident. My answer was, "I felt frightened." This, too, had changed. For the past few weeks, it had been, "I am frightened and cruel." The cruel piece had dropped away, as it should have.

What I did to Moki three years earlier was not done out of cruelty. It was done to correct a bad behavior. I tried everything I could think of, and the vet was pressuring me to fix it. In my desperation, I made a bad decision that changed both our lives. If only I had known then that becoming the pack leader would have solved the food aggression problem. Then, none of this would have happened. But I didn't know that.

Next, Ryan wanted to know a positive statement that I would like to believe about myself. It had been, "I am kind and courageous." Since "cruel" had come out of the negative statement, I didn't need "kind" anymore. But "courageous" didn't feel right to me, either. It was a scary situation! Of course I felt frightened! So, the positive statement was, "I want to react like any normal person would react."

After a few sets of quick eye movements, the vision of Moki's initial lunge dropped down to a one. Ryan then had me close my eyes and continue going through the scenario. The next part that bothered me was him jumping, biting, and backing me up. That one cleared up right away.

And finally, the last thing that bothered me was when he stopped biting and stood a few feet away with that scared look on his face. I knew I needed to get him into the house, and I did. I struggled to describe the emotion that I felt. Thinking about it, though, I came up with "competent." I knew what I had to do—get this frightened and aggressive dog into the house without getting bitten again—and I did it. I handled it well: I was "competent."

In discussing this last image with Ryan, I told him that I had to do that—get him into the house—because I didn't have a choice. But I did have a choice. I could have left him outside. The dog had just bitten me a conservative fifty times. Who would have blamed me for leaving him outside to fend for himself? No one. Instead, I did the right thing, the responsible thing, the loving thing. I was competent. Ryan thought this was very good! We were close to the end.

Neener, Neener!

Our new home had a carpeted staircase between the first and second floors. When I would start to go upstairs, Moki would dash in front of me and bound up the stairs. At the top, with his tail waving in the air, he would give me what I'd come to think of as the "neener, neener" look. Oops. I recognized the look. It wasn't at all threatening—it was a look like he had gotten one over on me. Moki had just told me that I'd done something wrong! So I wrote to Jade and asked if I needed to be the first one up the stairs.

When Jade wrote back, she said that I needed to be the first one up the stairs, or the first one through any narrow space or any kind of an entry area. She said that it shows him that I am claiming the area and that I am making it safe for both of us. She also said that I needed to give him permission to get in and out of the car. And before he jumps in, I should brush my hand on the seat, so my scent is there first.

Moki is so smart, he tells me when I've done something wrong before I realize it myself! Luckily he didn't realize he was acting so transparent and giving away his "advantage."

A Fiery Situation

There was a fireplace outside on the lawn close to the entrance to the passageway of my apartment at our former home in Colorado. As I drove home late one afternoon and approached my building, I saw the flames, the smoke curling upward, and people and dogs all around. However, Pete and a couple other dogs were inside the fenced yard. Cooper was running loose, though. And I knew that Moki could easily deem him dangerous because of guilt by association.

I backed my car into an open spot and opened the back door nearest to our passageway. Moki had been home alone all day, and I knew he needed to pee. After greeting him at the door, I slipped on his regular leash. The Gentle Leader had a really short leash attached to it. If I needed to shoo away the other dogs, the longer leash would prove more effective. Lastly, I put on my heavy winter gloves—just in case.

We walked briskly outside—no dogs close, thankfully—and I asked Moki to jump in the car. After taking our evening walk, we drove around for a while. When we arrived back home, the fire still burned, and there were still people and animals milling about. I backed into the parking space again and rushed Moki into the house. Another tense situation averted. And I had to give the neighbors credit for keeping Pete inside the yard.

Last EMDR Session

    I arrived at my last EMDR appointment and after telling Ryan about my progress, we started. When I visualized the extreme biting event and verbalized what I'd like to believe, it completely changed from the last session. We had come so far already that we started in a different place. My negative statement was, "I don't know how to handle my dog around other dogs," and what I'd like to believe was, "I can handle my dog so we can both be safe." And during what Ryan called the "reprocessing," my statements changed to, "Moki is getting better and so am I," and "Both of us are almost healed!" Later I said, "If Moki is unpredictable, I know how to handle it," and "The more we heal, the more predictable he will be." Several times during the session, my thoughts drifted away from what I should be visualizing. Ryan said that meant it's losing its hold on me. That was good.
    At one point during the session, my thoughts strayed to an incident that happened in grammar school. Although it still bothered me, I had no idea it was related to my fear issues. We worked on that awhile, which ultimately brought us back to Moki and the extreme biting incident. It's amazing how the mind works.

When we had almost finished the session—and our professional relationship—we talked about the workings of EMDR, and how it works with the body, the emotions, and cognition. That's why I had to visualize the incident, feel what part of the body was affected and how it made me feel, and what I'd like to believe about it. It was an incredible process that changed my life and saved my dog. Thank you, Ryan.

After eating lunch, I drove home and packed, packed, packed, and loaded the car in between packing. When a couple came late in the evening to pick up my bed and couch, my car was already completely loaded. My plan was to stay at a motel and then drive to my friend Jennifer's early the following morning to load her car. I forgot that Moki would be with me. I didn't feel right leaving him at the old apartment with almost nothing in it. Consequently, I needed to make room for him at the last minute. The space I found for him was tiny. He couldn't lie down on the short trip to town. But I figured it wasn't that bad for only twenty minutes.

I put Moki into the backseat in his allotted area. It was so small, it confused him. And I expected trouble. If I reached back over my shoulder to get the seat belt, I thought there was a good chance he would go ballistic. Instead, I reached back close to the floor trying to get the seat belt that way. He went ballistic, anyway. Although I am a seat belt fanatic, there wasn't much I could do. So, I drove.

Since I hadn't been certain that the people would come pick up the bed that day, I hadn't reserved a motel room. As I drove down the mountain toward town, I figured I had better find a motel that would definitely have a vacancy. Once I got out of the car, Moki might not let me back in. When I pulled into the chosen motel, I rolled Moki's window partway down, thinking that might make him feel that he had extra space and wasn't so vulnerable.

It worked. When I got back into the car after getting the key to our room, he didn't even growl. After driving the short distance to our room, I got out and then opened the door for him without trying to reach for the leash. Moki jumped out and was fine.

Next morning, I drove back up the mountain, sans seat belt. He acted normal in the daylight. I might have been able to put on the seat belt, but I was taking no chances. With all the moving and unstable energy, I didn't want to push him.

The Dangers of Sharing a Room

I packed and loaded the car all day. Talk about unstable energy—I was living it. The more I packed, the more I realized I had to pack. Although I intended to finish by six o'clock, time wore on and it got later and later. My dear friend, Jennifer, who was going to help me move, waited at a hotel that had a hot tub. The plan was to finish packing and then enjoy the hot tub while it soothed my muscles. Then we would leave early the next morning.

As I watched the clock, I kept in mind what time the hot tub closed. Since it would take an hour to get to the hotel, I knew eight o'clock was my deadline. At eight o'clock, I wasn't close to finishing. Time wore on. I kept stuffing items into the almost full car. This time I was careful to leave Moki plenty of room in the backseat. The drive to our new home would take six hours. Moki needed to feel comfortable.

I also wanted to leave his crate empty, so I could bring it into the hotel and have him sleep in it. Although he had really improved, I still didn't completely trust him around other people. But as the evening got later and later and the car got fuller and fuller, I started putting a few items into his crate which was already loaded in the car. At first, I thought it would be easy removing the few items and bringing the crate into the room. When more and more small items went into the crate, I realized that was not going to happen.

That's when I started to worry. What if Jennifer got up to go to the bathroom in the middle of the night? Would Moki bite her? I didn't know what to do. Jennifer lived only five minutes from the hotel and was only there for the hot tub and for leaving early the following morning. Would I be out of line if when I arrived there, whatever time that might be, I asked her to sleep at home for the night and meet in the morning?

Since I was uncomfortable with sharing the hotel room with someone when Moki was around, I had discussed the situation with Ryan in our last session. We agreed that I needed to verbalize my needs and Moki's needs to Jennifer. But it didn't feel acceptable asking Jennifer to leave when she was helping me move.

I had to come up with something else. Luckily I had hours to decide! I didn't finish packing the house and loading the car until after ten o'clock. Then I had an hour's drive to the hotel. That gave me plenty of time to think of options. On the drive over there, I came up with a reasonable plan.

Jennifer was already asleep when Moki and I arrived at the hotel hours and hours after our intended arrival. I came into the room and saw that she had chosen the bed by the door—also the bed closest to the desk. If I slept in the other bed, then Moki would be between Jennifer and the bathroom—not a safe option. Although I felt bad about it, I asked Jennifer if she would switch beds with me. Thankfully, she didn't mind. After attaching Moki's long leash to the desk, we all slept peacefully through the night.

I have to mention at this point that Jennifer thought it was me and my issues that provoked all of Moki's issues. So she had no fear of Moki. Next morning when Moki jumped on the bed and Jennifer sat beside him to pet him, he growled. It wasn't an out and out mean growl. It was more of a "mmmmmm." Still, it wasn't benevolent. I pulled Moki away from her, she stood up, and the incident ended. If that was the worst that happened between Jennifer and Moki during our moving experience, I knew I'd feel happy.

Meeting the Angel Dog Whisperer

Finally, it was time to meet Janice, my angel dog whisperer who had brought a miracle into my life. Since I had moved to Arizona, it was now a two-day drive to Boulder.

Janice and I both arrived in town—Janice by plane, and me and Moki by car. I met Jade, Janice, and John, Janice's eleven-year-old nephew, for dinner. Janice's service dog, Wyatt, stayed in the car.

Something that Janice said struck me. She said, "A dog trainer trains dogs. A dog whisperer, or dog behaviorist, changes dogs' behavior. And part of the program is changing the human's behavior." And that's exactly what I needed: someone to change Moki's—and my—behavior.

A Walk in the Park

The following morning, I had my first session with Janice. First, she corrected me for holding the leash in both hands. Jade had corrected me for that, too, but it was an old habit left over from obedience training. If I hold the leash in both hands, I am being consumed with the dog. My hand that holds the leash needs to be straight down. The dog is with me; I am not with the dog. I needed to stop worrying about what the dog was doing and take care of my own life. This wasn't just dog behavior instructions, this was advice about life!

I held my left arm (the one holding the leash) slightly elevated—still leftover from feeling afraid that Moki would bite my hand. Janice said that I needed to have my hand all the way down or in my pocket. She said that energy travels down the leash and up the leash. It's a circle of energy. If I was afraid, it would affect Moki's behavior.

As we walked the busy river path heading toward the park, I was to give Moki a gentle correction if he focused on anything besides walking straight ahead. There were kids and dogs everywhere. Moki wasn't the only one who needed to focus on walking straight ahead. But if he focused on something else, he was less able to know where I was. And since I was the pack leader, he needed to always be aware of where I was.

We walked all around the park. At one point, Janice directed us over to a tree to look at the new spring buds. She said if there is an uncomfortable situation, instead of pulling him back, walk away and look at something else. A mother and two children, including a toddler, walked by where we had just been. Janice said the toddler would have run right up to Moki if we hadn't moved.

"Why can't we just walk away instead of going to look at the tree?" I asked Janice.

"You want to focus on where you're going. You do not want to focus on why you're leaving. If you're focused on getting away from something uncomfortable or scary, you will have fearful, negative energy." I understood that perfectly. Positive energy brings positive results.

Our next obstacle was a boisterous homeless man who Moki wasn't happy with at all. Moki could feel the man's unstable energy. Janice deflected the man's attention while Moki and I found another tree to look at!

Out of nowhere, a loose dog started meandering our way. Before I had a chance to feel anxious, Janice approached the dog and with a quick "sshhh," sent him off in another direction.

Later, we sat on a bench while dogs and people walked by us. Although I was nervous, I knew Janice would avert any possible danger before it affected Moki. While we walked and while we sat on the bench, Janice imparted all kinds of dog whisperer wisdom. Our meeting with Janice was informative and rewarding. When I got back to my hotel room, I tried to write it all down so I wouldn't forget.

At the Pet Store

After lunch, we all drove to a pet store to do a demonstration so Jade could get more clients. When Janice asked me to go with them and bring Moki, I didn't realize that I would be part of the demonstration!

Since we had two cars, I found a parking place quickly, and Moki and I walked across the street to the pet store. One experience that I longed for was to walk down the street with Moki and not have to worry about him biting people. And there we were, walking down the street. Although I felt worried about it, my fear level was low. But I did hope that no one stuck out his or her hand to pet Moki without asking.

We made it safely down the street, then sat on a bench in front of the pet store and waited. People passed by, and I hoped no one would notice us. Dogs passed by on leash, and I held my breath. Someone with a dog wanted to let their dog sniff noses with Moki, and I said no. A couple stopped to admire my beautiful dog. When Moki wagged his tail, I let them pet him. He didn't bite them! That gave me more confidence. As I knew from the beginning, it wasn't a danger of Moki biting someone. It was my fear of Moki biting someone. A fear that had become more and more absurd. Yet, I still wasn't ready to let it go.

After what felt like hours but was only minutes, Jade, Janice, and John came into view. They walked into the pet store and invited me in. I'm not sure what I expected, but walking into a busy pet store with people and animals milling around was not it. And yet, Janice told me to come in. Since I trusted Janice, Moki and I walked inside.

Here I was: the woman whose dog bit her fifty times and she lived to tell about it. And here was her dog: acting perfectly normal. We were a success story!

As I walked in, I saw Janice by the counter already talking to the owner. A large, brown, square-faced, furry dog rested his front feet on the gate next to her as he barked wildly at Moki. With my lesson learned, I immediately pulled Moki behind me. Janice sshhhed the dog, and it stopped barking. Another scary situation averted.

I stood in place with Moki at my side, because I didn't know what else to do. A few minutes later, the owner of the pet store handed Janice a leash with a black and white shaggy dog attached. The dog looked at Moki. Moki looked at the dog. I felt unsure what I should do, so I let Moki take a couple steps forward, but I kept the leash taut. Janice said I should decide to keep him with me or to let him sniff the dog. Keeping the leash taut was not an option.

Reluctantly, I let the leash out. Moki, while wagging his tail, walked slowly toward the shaggy dog. They sniffed noses. They wagged tails. After a few minutes, the tension got to me, so I pulled Moki back. Nothing had occurred to make me afraid. It was completely my fear and had nothing to do with Moki.

When some new people walked in with their dogs, Moki and I walked toward the back of the pet store. When the coast was clear, we'd amble toward the front. Then the owner of the store approached me. When he asked if he could pet Moki, I hesitated. Janice said, "How about if you walk him, instead." She gently took the leash from me and handed it to the man. He walked Moki around the store, past a couple other dogs, and then walked him back to me. Success!

Again, it reinforced my knowledge that most of Moki's problem was me. After more time passed, John came up and asked if he could pet Moki. Janice handed him the leash, and he walked Moki around with no problem. Moki was fine.

More dogs came into the store, and Moki and I wandered toward the back again. Some of the dogs wagged their tails, and Moki wagged back. I allowed Moki to go a limited distance toward them, but with the leash taut. Janice reminded me to make a decision. It was not an easy decision to make, because this was the situation that scared me. But I knew which way I *should* decide, so I let Moki walk toward the other dogs. Everything turned out fine.

It was almost closing time. Moki and I were still in the back of the store. The owner opened the gate and let another dog out. This was another black and white shaggy dog, but much bigger than the first one. All the dogs up to this point had been on leash. This one was not. When I saw it look our way, I walked Moki around a treat stand at the back of the store. When we again faced the front, the dog had become interested in something else. This happened several times, but the dog never approached all the way.

While this was happening, Janice was at the counter talking on the phone. The big, shaggy dog looked our way again. Before I had time to walk Moki away, Janice, still on the phone, stepped between us and the dog and sshhhed it away. She said to me, "I have your back. And you need to show Moki that you have his." Thank you, Janice.

When we arrived back at the hotel, Janice asked me to follow her. She took my hand and pulled me so I was right next to her. Then, she proceeded to walk me straight into a trash can! She said, "Don't do that to Moki." We walked back several paces, and she held my hand again, but looser this time. We walked by the trash can again. That time, I had enough leeway to walk behind her, thus avoiding the trash can. Janice said, "This is what you need to do with Moki. Walk where you want to walk, and he will follow."

Upstairs in Janice's room, I wanted to go over some of her advice from the day's lessons. She started by saying that in any situation I find myself in with Moki, I have these choices: fight, flight, avoid, or submit. Something that I needed to do was to give myself permission to avoid. Because even avoiding was taking charge, and that's what Moki needed me to do. If I felt uncomfortable, then I should walk Moki away. Janice said that if I don't want to be a victim, then do something. She said it's important not to pull back on the leash when I'm afraid—that is unstable energy. Just walk away.

Janice said that the old me was very fearful. She said that I needed to take charge without being fearful. I needed to walk away without being fearful. She said fearful dogs react to fearful owners. To make Moki more predictable, *I* had to become more predictable—more stable. And if I wanted Moki to trust my judgment, *I* had to trust my judgment. The more stable I become, the more stable he would become.

Janice said that it's important that I don't talk to Moki after I correct him. Talking is reward and excitement. Also, if I look at him, Moki could perceive that as a challenge to him. She said it's like when you're in a movie theater and the person behind you is talking on their cell phone. You turn around and say, "Sshhh," but you don't continue staring at them to see if they'll comply.

Before the end of the evening, Janice asked me, "Are you an angry person?"

I answered, "No."

She said "But you do get angry, right?" After I nodded my head, she continued. "Moki is not an aggressive dog. But he can be aggressive."

A Little Excitement

Our caravan consisted of Jade driving with Janice, John, and Wyatt (Janice's service dog) in her car, and me and Moki following in my car. We headed toward Fort Collins to have dinner with Janice's good friend, Temple Grandin. We stopped at a western store. John and I looked at belts for a while, and then I went back to the car to get Moki. We walked around and tried to find some shade.

Then I put him in the car and went back into the western store to see if Janice had finished. Since she was still looking around, I returned to the car and John followed. As we stood beside my car, I pointed to the windows and said, "Although it's hot out, I can't leave the windows rolled down very much. That's why I don't leave him in the car by himself very long."

John, a brilliant and precocious preteen said, "In my opinion, you should roll the windows down to here." As he spoke, he ran his fingers along the window two inches below where I had it. Moki snarled and went into instant attack mode. It surprised me and John, and we quickly backed away from him.

Moki had triggered my fear button. I knew I had to get him out of the car to calm us both down. Also, I did not want to get into the car with him in that mood. After waiting a few minutes, I opened the door. Instead of reaching inside, I allowed him to jump out of the car before I grabbed the leash. With him outside the car, I didn't feel like he was a danger.

We walked around for a few minutes. Although I felt scared, Moki was fine. Janice and Jade walked out of the western store. I approached them and told Janice what had happened. When we reached my car, Janice stopped and looked around. Two dogs barked loudly from the back of a truck thirty feet away. Janice asked, "Were they barking when this happened?"

I answered, "Yes."

She said, "Then that's where the unstable energy came from." Then she noticed that I had the regular leash on him, and she asked, "Can you put on the Gentle Leader?"

"No," I said, "I'm too afraid." Janice held out her hand for me to give her the Gentle Leader. I pulled Moki toward me and said, "I don't want him to bite you."

She said emphatically, "I don't care!" Janice has been bitten more than a thousand times, by her own account. My guess is that that is a conservative number. A few days before when I had first met her, she wore a bandage on her hand from her latest dog bite. It wasn't healed yet.

Janice took the leash from me, and we walked Moki around. With my fear piqued, I bent my arm at the elbow as I walked beside Moki, so my hand wouldn't be within biting range. Then, Janice asked me to stay behind, and she walked Moki toward the truck with the barking dogs. As she passed by them, she sshhhed the dogs. Janice and Moki made a wide circle around the barking dogs. When they walked between two cars at a spot where Moki could see me, he looked to make sure I was still there. They continued walking the circle around the barking dogs, with Janice sshhhing them at every round, and Moki watching for me each time.

Moki settled, and Janice handed me back the leash. She said, "Moki did great! He could have redirected his fear at me and bitten me, but he didn't. He's fine!"

Although I felt too scared to put on the Gentle Leader, my fear only felt like a two instead of the eight or ten that it might have been before. Taking him out of the backseat after he snarled at John would have almost incapacitated me before, but I did it, and it hardly bothered me. I realized that I had made much progress in the previous two months.

Lessons from the Dog Whisperer

Back in Janice's hotel room after dinner, I talked to Jade while Janice made a phone call. I had written down what I thought were the three most important lessons for *me* to remember, and I wanted to go over them. Jade helped me. Number one: Keep the leash in one hand. A simple lesson, but one I needed constant reminding of. Number two: When Moki shows too much interest in something while we're walking, give him a quick sshhh to redirect his focus. Number three: If I find we are in an uncomfortable situation, instead of pulling on the leash, I should walk away and put our attention on something else.

After Janice finished her phone conversation, she came into the room and sat down. Her service dog, the number one service dog in the United States (!), Wyatt the Rhodesian Ridgeback, lay on the floor in the middle of the room. Janice told me to pick up the wastebasket that was on the other side of Wyatt. The idea was for me to "walk through" Wyatt—to walk in such a manner that Wyatt would get up so I could retrieve the wastebasket. Janice said that it's basic respect. If the energy is strong enough, the dog will immediately get up. If there is a purpose to my wanting to walk that way, he will get out of my way.

I walked up to Wyatt and stopped short. I couldn't do it. Wyatt didn't move. My energy wasn't strong enough to move a mouse, let alone a ninety-pound Rhodesian Ridgeback.

After my epic failure, Janice said that it's important for Moki to realize "It's not my floor. It's my mom's floor." Janice said that I should not look down at Moki when I'm walking through. Just walk. She said a pack leader would not stand up to get out of the way of one of its pack members. But a pack member better get out of the way for the pack leader. I should not be concerned where my dog is. My dog needs to be aware of where I am and show respect by moving. If I'm walking toward him, he should automatically get out of my way.

Janice felt the reason I had a difficult time "walking through" was because of my apprehension in wanting to take over the role of pack leader. She thought that I wasn't comfortable enough to just do it. Either because I didn't think I was worthy of being my dog's pack leader, or perhaps because I was afraid of not being loved if I was pack leader.

That did strike a note of truth in me. I don't like to admit this, and I don't like it about myself, but I do have elements of being a "people pleaser" in my personality. I want everyone to like me. I don't like to do anything or present myself in any way that would make people not want to be my friend. Many years ago when I worked at a school, the kids in my class ran all over me because I didn't want to be the "bad guy" and discipline them. I wanted to be their friend. That didn't work out!

But it was Moki's job to follow my rules. I can't feel guilty about that. I'm not being mean—I'm allowing him to follow his purpose, which is being a dog. Janice said that if a dog feels you're not doing your job—being the pack leader—he will take over. And Moki sees everything as black and white. Either I'm the pack leader or I'm not. Dogs won't follow unstable energy. So if I'm weak, he will take over.

I need to stop taking everything personally. And I need to be confident enough to give him the comfort of knowing that I am in charge and I will take care of him. If I allow it, Moki will make me a stronger person. Then the "aha" moment: If I want Moki not to be afraid, I can't be afraid. That's the essence of it all, isn't it?

Be the Pack Leader

The following evening we all drove to a different part of town so Janice could watch Jade give a class. After parking in the large parking lot, Janice walked over to my car. She wanted to see how "car aggressive" Moki was. Moki hit the window so hard, I thought he bruised his muzzle. Janice walked around the car, and Moki barked as she approached either of his two windows. He would go for her and then back off, then go for her again when she approached the opposite window. When she walked away, he immediately stopped.

Janice said that was good. Some dogs would keep barking for fifteen minutes after you walk away, but Moki's heart wasn't in it. Although fear and protectiveness can go together, she felt Moki was not as fearful as he was uncertain. Should I do this or shouldn't I? Fearful dogs are normally fearful in every situation, but Moki wasn't like that. And that was good news.

After Janice's session with Moki, we walked over to Jade's new client. Jade had met the man at work when he briefly left his little white dog outside. The dog barked the whole time he was gone. So, his dog not only had major separation anxiety but also a few other issues, including: peeing in his house at night if allowed loose, humping the cat, and when the dog was on the bed, it would growl at him and his girlfriend. They were different problems than I had with Moki, and yet, the solution was the same: Be the pack leader.

A Growl is Not Always a Growl

Back in Arizona in our new home, I had just bought a couch with recliners on each end. I started pulling out one recliner, and Moki got in the way. Since he didn't cry out, I wasn't sure if it hurt him or just scared him. But he growled low and raised his tail and his hackles. He had that "ready to take the offensive" look about him. I didn't think fast enough to "sshhhh" him, but I sent him to his crate. A few minutes later, I invited him out to go get his ball. He ran out of the crate bouncy and happy.

It turned out that I learned much from this incident. My fear stayed at a low level the whole time. And although I didn't react correctly (by sshhhing him), I did react acceptably. Moki forgot about it immediately, as expected, and we returned to our happy life together.

Or so I thought. Later that afternoon as we played together, Moki growled. It was "just" his playing growl, but I thought that I shouldn't allow it. I knew that his growl that sounded like ru-ru-ru was okay. But I thought that I should correct for the plain kind—even if it's meant in fun. So, I sshhhed him. It confused him. His tail drooped, and he looked like he wasn't sure of what was going on. We played more—he growled again, and I sshhhed him again. I could tell that he felt confused. The situation made my energy unstable.

Shortly after that, I needed to take him outside. When I tried to put on his Gentle Leader, it didn't go right on like it usually does. My unstable energy got the best of me, and I couldn't do it. After a few more minutes, I put the regular leash on him, and we walked outside. We weren't as healed as I had thought. It was a long process, though. I had to keep reminding myself of that.

Healing Together

I wrote to Janice about the growling and Moki's confusion. She told me what I expected her to tell me—what Moki told me with his confusion—I shouldn't have corrected his growling. Janice said I should correct the "This is my toy. It's all mine, and you can't have it" growl. I knew that growl. Moki often did it after I gave him a new toy. But that was not the growl that I corrected the day before. That's why it confused Moki. Since *he* knew it was just a play growl, he didn't understand why I corrected him. Moki was smart enough to know when he did something wrong. And he usually told me. I wrote back to Janice that maybe Moki could be one of her teachers!

Something else that Janice said in her email was that we're not trying to make him an unhappy, boring dog. We should still have fun together and bond. I just took it a little too far—in trying to do the right thing. Sometimes the whole process confused me, and I wasn't sure whether to correct or not to correct. Or I should say, to sshhh or not to sshhh! I needed to learn to trust Moki's signals. He was very good at telling me when he needed correction—his "neener, neener" look—and when he didn't need it—when he raised his hackles because he didn't understand why I corrected him. But I still didn't feel sure enough—of either of us. That's why I needed to check in with Janice or Jade when something like this happened.

A side effect of the growling/wrong correction/hackle incident was that it brought back some of my fear. It wasn't gone yet. I had to remember what Ryan had told me—it was up to me to push down unreasonable fears. So when the fear cropped up again and made me afraid to pet him, I confirmed to myself that I didn't want to be afraid anymore. Then I pushed the fear down to a point five, and embraced Moki as if nothing had happened. It worked. We would heal together. And we would be fine.

Epilogue

When I started the whole healing process, I thought that EMDR would be a "magic pill" for me, and that the dog whisperer would be a "magic pill" for Moki. And once each of us had our respective magic pill, it would cure us immediately and forever. But after we returned from our meeting with Janice, and the recliner issue scared Moki into giving me a defensive growl, I realized that we weren't finished yet.

Janice said there would still be challenges with him, like teenagers continue to challenge their parents. She said the difference now was that I have the tools to correct it, so it won't be a problem. There hadn't been another incident since the couch. But I knew if there was another challenge, I would know what to do, and we would be okay.

A thought occurred to me. Back in the bad old days, when Moki was afraid of me and I was afraid of him, I remember thinking that if he ever bit me in the face, then that would be it. There would be no way I could keep him after that. Then, after the extreme biting event happened, I remember thinking that as bad as it was, considering that he bit my gloves instead of my bare hands, it was a much better outcome than getting bitten in the face. And it would serve the same purpose: I couldn't keep him. But, my new thought—after the dog whisperer and the EMDR—was that even if something really terrible happened and Moki bit me in the face, I would not give him up.

Moki may not be completely healed yet. I may not be completely healed yet. Knowing that I will keep him regardless of what happens, means to me that he and I are both healed enough for now. The healing will continue. Love has triumphed.

Resources

Resources

Dog Whisperers (Animal Behaviorists)

United K9 Professionals
http://www.unitedk9professionals.com
Training@UnitedK9Professionals.com
201-788-3882 1-855-4k9pros

Jade Selvy
Jades@unitedk9professionals.com

Horse Whisperer

Frank Bell
http://www.horsewhisperer.com/
info@horsewhisperer.com

Service Dogs

Merlin's Kids
http://www.merlinskids.org/
Janice@unitedk9professionals.com
201-788-3882

EMDR

EMDR Institute, Inc.
http://www.emdr.com/

EMDR International Association
http://www.emdria.org/

Other Books by Jerri Kay Lincoln

Children's Books

Why Do Puppy Dogs Have Cold Noses?
Cooper's Smile
The Little Unicorn Who Could*
The Invisible Lion
Do Bears Poop in the Woods?*
Can Pigs Fly?*

* Also available as a coloring book

The Unicorn Wisdom Series

The Unicorn Whisperer
Dancing with Unicorns

Yoga Books

Exercises for Therapeutic Riding
Easy Airplane Yoga
Wheelchair Yoga
Yoga on Horseback
Bathroom Yoga

Check out the Doggie Blog to keep track of Jerri and Moki:

http://www.jerrilincoln.com/doggieblog.html

Ralston Store Publishing
Prescott, Arizona

www.ingramcontent.com/pod-product-compliance
Lightning Source LLC
Chambersburg PA
CBHW061646040426
42446CB00010B/1604